Path to Stellar Business Performance Analysis

A Design and Implementation Handbook

Suvradeep Bhattacharjee

Path to Stellar Business Performance Analysis: A Design and Implementation Handbook

Suvradeep Bhattacharjee
Cambridge, UK

ISBN-13 (pbk): 979-8-8688-1500-3   ISBN-13 (electronic): 979-8-8688-1501-0
https://doi.org/10.1007/979-8-8688-1501-0

Copyright © 2025 by Suvradeep Bhattacharjee

Managing Director, Apress Media LLC: Welmoed Spahr
Acquisitions Editor: Shivangi Ramachandran
Development Editor: James Markham
Editorial Assistant: Jessica Vakili

Cover designed by eStudioCalamar

Distributed to the book trade worldwide by Springer Science+Business Media New York, 1 New York Plaza, New York, NY 10004. Phone 1-800-SPRINGER, fax (201) 348-4505, e-mail orders-ny@springer-sbm.com, or visit www.springeronline.com. Apress Media, LLC is a Delaware LLC and the sole member (owner) is Springer Science + Business Media Finance Inc (SSBM Finance Inc). SSBM Finance Inc is a **Delaware** corporation.

For information on translations, please e-mail booktranslations@springernature.com; for reprint, paperback, or audio rights, please e-mail bookpermissions@springernature.com.

Apress titles may be purchased in bulk for academic, corporate, or promotional use. eBook versions and licenses are also available for most titles. For more information, reference our Print and eBook Bulk Sales web page at http://www.apress.com/bulk-sales.

Any source code or other supplementary material referenced by the author in this book is available to readers on GitHub. For more detailed information, please visit https://www.apress.com/gp/services/source-code.

If disposing of this product, please recycle the paper

To my wife, Sunrita, and daughter, Rai.

Table of Contents

About the Author

 **Suvradeep Bhattacharjee** is an accomplished analyst who has insights into using and developing web-based products. Skilled in improving product and business performance, Suvradeep has previously worked with the UK Cabinet Office, IBM, CGI, and the United States Air Force. Suvradeep is a keen gardener and an aspiring mathematician. In his leisure, he follows Monty Don and Johann Carl Friedrich Gauss, not necessarily in that order.

Introduction

A writer only begins a book. A reader finishes it.

—Samuel Johnson

This book will help you finish carving a path to stellar business performance analysis. By capturing the right performance measures, collecting data from those measures, analyzing performance data, and improving products and processes based on that analysis, you will be in a position to put your business on a stellar performance trajectory after finishing this book. This book serves as a design and implementation guide for Senior Leaders, Product Managers, Product Owners, Web Analytics Professionals, and UX Professionals who are trying to navigate the business performance analysis maze.

The book has three sections: (1) the design of a performance analysis function (Chapters 1, 2, 3), (2) the implementation of a performance analysis function (Chapters 4, 5), and (3) product and business improvement using UX design principles (Chapters 6, 7).

The first chapter is titled "Vision, Goals, Objectives, and Pursuit of Product Innovation." This chapter launches the design of the Business Performance Analysis function, by introducing three important building blocks, that is, vision-goals-objectives. To determine which metrics to measure for a particular product, one needs to understand which set of Performance Measures really matters for the performance of that specific product. Also, product objectives define which measures really matter. In retrospect, product objectives are product goals with targets. Finally, product goals flow from the overarching product vision. Therefore, product vision emerges as the obvious starting topic of this book.

The second chapter is titled "Setting Up Performance Measures." This chapter outlines a blueprint for selecting, defining, and measuring what is important for each product performance and the overall business performance. Performance is a complex concept, especially when it comes to understanding business performance. The need to critically examine and define what constitutes firm performance and how firm performance can be measured is increasingly evident in today's fiercely competitive business landscape. In recent years, the idea of performance has gained prominence, often being touted as a primary focus for organizations striving for excellence. Many companies assert that they are dedicated to enhancing their performance and actively seek to establish performance measures to evaluate their achievements. However, despite this focus on performance, there remains a pervasive sense of dissatisfaction with the current performance measurement systems employed by many organizations. A substantial number of firms—potentially even a majority—believe that their performance measurement frameworks are inadequate.

The third chapter is titled "Setting up Performance Frameworks and Creating Blueprints for Success." This chapter outlines a roadmap for setting up Performance Frameworks. Setting up Performance Frameworks is pivotal to accomplishing stellar business performance. However, implementing effective performance frameworks, like the Balanced Scorecard, does not guarantee better organizational performance, as strategy execution is a big anathema for managers. Why is that true? A common issue is incorrect assumptions about the validity of a firm's business model, which plagues most organizations.

KPIs and Performance Frameworks are continually in search of the right display tools. Google Analytics, which is by far the most popular, is the chosen display tool. Chapter 4, titled "Analyzing Business Performance with Google Analytics," deals with implementation details of a business performance analysis function. Chapter 5, titled "Deep Dive into Google Analytics Data Visualization," provides an in-depth account of implementation of performance analysis using Google Analytics Data Visualization. The quest for a visualization tool is, in essence, the quest for incisive insights.

The last two chapters, Chapter 6 and Chapter 7, focus on measuring user behavior and improving business performance. Senior managers and key stakeholders typically focus on performance metrics, particularly when presented well. They are interested in how many users can successfully complete essential tasks with a product. These performance metrics are viewed as significant indicators of usability and potential predictors of cost savings and revenue growth.

CHAPTER 1

Vision, Goals, Objectives, and Pursuit of Product Innovation

The pursuit of stellar business performance is not easy. To achieve stellar business performance, senior leadership must understand, measure, and improve good performance. For product centric businesses, good business performance is a function of good performances of their portfolio of products. Therefore, measuring product performance is pivotal to measure and improve overall business performance.

Measuring product performance is not an easy feat either. To determine which metrics to measure for a particular product, one needs to understand which set of Performance Measures really matters for the performance of that specific product. Also, product objectives define which measures really matter. In retrospect, product objectives are product goals with targets. Finally, product goals flow from the overarching product vision. Therefore, product vision emerges as the obvious starting topic of this book.

© Suvradeep Bhattacharjee 2025
S. Bhattacharjee, *Path to Stellar Business Performance Analysis*,
https://doi.org/10.1007/979-8-8688-1501-0_1

Vision

We know what we are but know not what we may be.

—William Shakespeare

So, what is a vision? Figure 1-1 addresses the question of vision:

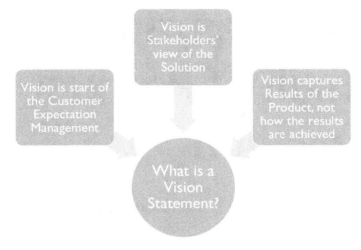

Figure 1-1. *What is a Vision Statement*

Vision statement should capture results of a product and should refrain from indicating how the results are achieved. Vision is essentially all the stakeholders' view of the solution which is achieved when the product solves a plethora of customer problems or, at least, a customer problem. Most importantly, vision statement is the start of the customer expectation management journey which, at the outset, sets the customer expectation from the product.

Customer expectation is set by articulating the problems the product will solve and the future state the product will deliver after the product solves those customer problems. This is captured in Figures 1-2 through 1-4.

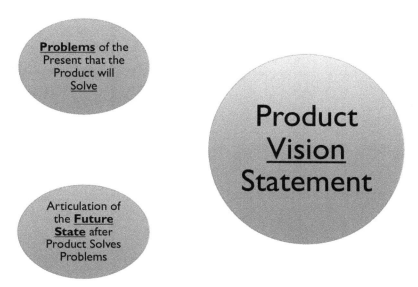

Figure 1-2. *What is a Product Vision Statement*

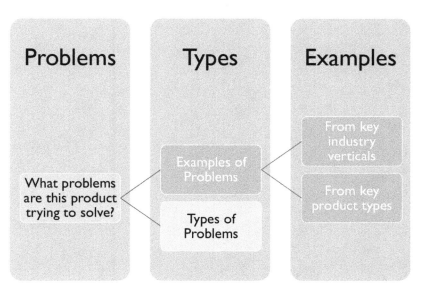

Figure 1-3. *What problems is this product trying to solve?*

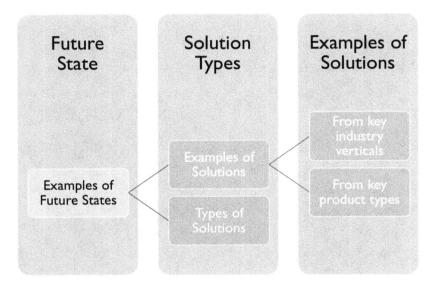

Figure 1-4. *Examples of Future States*

Table 1-1 lists my analysis of Visions of world-leading organizations.

Table 1-1. Visions of World-Leading Organizations

Company	Industry vertical	Vision statement	Future state	Problems of the present	Planned solution
Netflix	Media	Helping content creators around the world to find a global audience	Global audience captured	Lack of global reach for content creators	Netflix app provides access to a global audience.
Disney	Media	To make people happy	Happy audience	Unhappy audience	Disney content products bringing happiness to its audience
Google	Technology	To organize world's information and make it universally accessible and useful.	World's information organized, accessible, useful	World's information is poorly organized, inaccessible, and not very useful.	Google search engine and other products help organize world's information.
Apple	Technology	To make the best products on earth and to leave the world better than we found it	Apple making the best products on earth and making the world better	Existing products are not bringing the best user experience.	Best user experiences are delivered through Apple's products.

(continued)

Table 1-1. (*continued*)

Company	Industry vertical	Vision statement	Future state	Problems of the present	Planned solution
IBM	Technology	To be the world's most successful and important information technology company. Successful in helping our customers apply technology to solve their problems. Successful in introducing this extraordinary technology to new customers. Important because we will continue to be the basic resource of much of what is invested in this industry.	IBM becoming the world's most successful and important IT company.	To solve existing and new customers' problems.	Apply Information Technology to solve customer problems.

Ikea	Retail	Create better everyday lives for as many people as possible.	Better lives, every day.	Everyday lives of many people could be improved.	Ikea's products would make lives better for many people.
Amazon	Retail	To be the world's most customer-centric company	Amazon – most customer-centric company in the world	Amazon is not the most customer-centric company in the world.	Amazon's products and services would make it the most customer-centric company in the world by supplying any product a customer might want to buy online.
Mercedes	Automotive	We will build the world's most desirable cars.	Mercedes cars are the world's most desirable cars.	Mercedes cars are not the world's most desirable cars.	Mercedes would build cars which would be most desirable in the world.
Rolls Royce	Automotive	Inspiring Greatness	Rolls Royce makes great products that inspire greatness.	It is hard to inspire. It is harder to inspire greatness.	Rolls Royce cars and engines would delight customers and inspire greatness.
GE	Manufacturing	To be number 1 or 2 in every single market we serve.	GE is either number 1 or 2 in every market it serves.	GE is not number 1 or 2 in all the markets it serves.	GE would become number 1 or 2 in every market it serves through its products and services.

Goals and Objectives

Our doubts are traitors and make us lose the good we oft might win, by fearing to attempt.

—William Shakespeare

Creation of product goals is a very important milestone. This milestone is achieved by drawing on the vision statement elements such as expected results. This is captured in Figure 1-5.

Figure 1-5. *How to create Product Goals*

Goals can be split further into product goals and product improvement goals. This is captured in Figure 1-6.

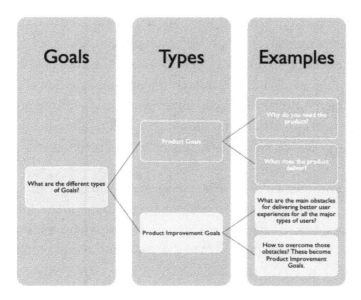

Figure 1-6. *Product Goals and Product Improvement Goals*

Stellar business performance is built by stellar products. Stellar products come in a variety of shapes and forms, but one element is common among them, that is, innovation. Without a discourse on product innovation, any narrative of stellar business performance will be fatally flawed.

Product Innovation

Innovation comes from saying no to a thousand things

—Steve Jobs

Linking business strategy with innovation strategy is critical for any business to succeed and have a stellar performance. Understanding the innovation management of a company is of paramount importance in a quest for stellar business performance. Therefore, we would explore how a robust innovation strategy can lead to stellar business performance.

There are two types of new products: one, new to the company, and two, new to the market. Some new product projects take a company into unfamiliar territory—a product category new to the firm, new customers with unfamiliar needs, unfamiliar technology, new sales force, channels and servicing requirements, or an unfamiliar manufacturing process. Step-out projects are riskier and have higher failure rates due to a lack of strengths, experience, knowledge, and skills. And the business often pays the price.

To avert product failure, each and every stage of the product innovation process must have a razor-sharp customer focus. Innovative project teams should build a series of iterative steps where successive versions of the product are shown to the customer to seek feedback and verification.

Product Ideation

If at first, the idea is not absurd, then there is no hope for it.

—Albert Einstein

Effective product ideation is central to success of a new product project. Time tested effective product ideation methods are:

- Lead user analysis where information is collected about needs and solutions from the leading users of the target market and from markets facing similar problems in a more extreme form. This ideation method is used for developing breakthrough products. This voice of the customer method captures the expert customer data, leading to fine design criteria.

- Focus groups.

- Intervention by customer visit teams.

- Assessing what disruptive technologies can offer in terms of building new products.

Product Innovation Management Framework

The only way you can increase the size of the pie, which is the firm revenue, and, the market size, is by innovating in new products. According to the Product Development and Management Association (PDMA), successful high-technology companies have found that more than 50% of their current sales are coming from new products (Barczak et al. 2009). Therefore, a company's innovation capabilities will determine its future growth potential.

Developing an innovation management framework is central to any good innovation strategy. A good innovation management framework comprises three key elements: first the level, second the dimensions, and third the competencies. Level could be on the firm level, it could be set on the industry level and it could be on the macro environment level. Crucial part of the innovation management framework are the dimensions, and the dimensions are (1) strategy, (2) organization and culture, (3) processes, (4) techniques and tools, and (5) metrics. There are five distinct competency areas: first is idea management, second market management, third portfolio management, fourth platform management, and, finally, fifth project management.

(Source: The PDMA handbook for Innovation and New Product Development)

Firms have invested substantial resources in becoming leaner and more agile. The pursuit of productivity, quality, and speed has produced a plethora of management tools and techniques such as total quality management (TQM), reengineering, outsourcing, Six Sigma. However, these tools and techniques have failed to translate gains into sustainable, profitable growth which is absolutely important for the longer-term survival of many firms. Also, the products and services of these firms are very similar. Blow by blow, these tools and techniques have taken these firms farther away from strong competitive positions.

On the contrary, properly used performance measures can propel many firms to heights of longer-term success. There are a variety of metrics which organizations use to measure their innovation proficiency. Customer metrics such as market share growth and customer loyalty are often complemented by operational metrics such as time to profit and knowledge metrics, such as the number of patents. Most importantly, metrics chosen by the firm should be aligned with its innovation strategy. If a firm's strategic objective is to be the first to market, measuring traditional cycle times is totally unnecessary. In this case, the firm should focus on measuring the number of times the company is first to market.

Also, employee compensation must be tied to the innovation performance results. Many organizations invest substantial resources benchmarking best practices, designing, and documenting an innovation process, then leave the employee reward systems unconnected to the innovation process. It's no wonder that business performance doesn't improve; employees know that innovation really doesn't count toward a higher pay.

Setting up Performance Measures for Product innovation would help an organization to measure the effectiveness of their innovation strategy. Therefore, the development of product innovation performance measures such as product innovation KPIs is key to an organization's success. This topic of developing effective performance measures will be discussed in detail in Chapter 2, "Setting Up Performance Measures."

Summary

This chapter essentially discusses four strands that prepare the ground for a thorough performance analysis—vision, goals, objectives, and innovation. The first three strands are intertwined as product objectives define which measures really matter. In retrospect, product objectives are product goals with targets, and product goals flow from the vision statement element – expected results. You can visualize the fourth strand—innovation—as a tangent which touches the first three strands and defines what the best practices are.

So, what are the best practices? First principle: the only way you can increase the size of the pie, which is the firm revenue, and, the market size, is by innovating in new products. Second principle: a company's innovation capabilities will determine its future growth potential. Third principle: setting up Performance Measures for Product innovation would help an organization to measure the effectiveness of their innovation strategy. Therefore, the development of product innovation performance measures such as product innovation KPIs is key to an organization's success.

CHAPTER 2

Setting Up Performance Measures

Performance is a complex concept, especially when it comes to understanding business performance. The need to critically examine and define what constitutes firm performance and how firm performance can be measured is increasingly evident in today's fiercely competitive business landscape. In recent years, the idea of performance has gained prominence, often being touted as a primary focus for organizations striving for excellence. Many companies assert that they are dedicated to enhancing their performance and actively seek to establish performance measures to evaluate their achievements.

However, despite this focus on performance, there remains a pervasive sense of dissatisfaction with the current performance measurement systems employed by many organizations. A substantial number of firms—potentially even a majority—believe that their performance measurement frameworks are inadequate.

One contributing factor to this widespread discontent is the lack of effective non-financial indicators such as customer service excellence, the effectiveness of research and development initiatives, product quality upon first delivery, and ongoing employee development efforts.

© Suvradeep Bhattacharjee 2025
S. Bhattacharjee, *Path to Stellar Business Performance Analysis*,
https://doi.org/10.1007/979-8-8688-1501-0_2

Types of Performance Measures

Performance measures come in four different varieties:

1. Result Indicators (RI)

2. Key Result Indicators (KRI)

3. Performance Indicators (PI)

4. Key Performance Indicators (KPI)

Key Performance Indicators (KPIs) are essential tools for operating managers. They provide them with advance warning signals that can indicate potential challenges or problems that may arise in the future. These signals are crucial as they help managers understand which proactive actions need to be taken to mitigate risks and enhance overall performance.

It is important to differentiate between leading performance measures, which are represented by KPIs, and lagging performance measures, which are captured by Key Result Indicators (KRIs). KPIs focus on predictive metrics that can drive performance improvements, while KRIs reflect outcomes that have already occurred.

Leading performance measures include metrics related to production efficiency, employee engagement, or sales pipeline activity, enabling managers to foresee issues and act accordingly before they affect the organization. In contrast, lagging performance measures represent the results of actions taken, encompassing metrics such as customer satisfaction, net profit before tax, profit per customer, employee satisfaction, and return on capital employed. These lagging indicators provide valuable insights into how the organization has performed over a specific period, helping managers evaluate their strategies and make informed decisions for future planning.

By utilizing both KPIs and KRIs effectively, managers can maintain a comprehensive understanding of their organization's performance and ensure they remain on track to achieve their strategic goals.

Key Result Indicators (KRIs) and Key Performance Indicators (KPIs) serve distinct purposes within an organization's framework and should be treated as separate entities. This clear differentiation is crucial because it significantly improves the quality and clarity of performance reporting.

Managers can benefit from this separation by distinguishing between two critical categories of performance metrics. The first category encompasses metrics that directly influence top-level governance, providing insight into the organization's strategic goals and overall health. In contrast, the second category, the KPIs, consists of metrics that pertain to day-to-day management operations, helping to track the efficiency and effectiveness of ongoing activities.

To implement this structured approach, an organization should develop a comprehensive governance dashboard. This dashboard should ideally feature seven to nine high-level KRIs, which are essential for the board's oversight and decision-making processes. These KRIs should capture key aspects of organizational performance and risk to provide a snapshot of performance at the strategic level.

Organizations should complement the governance dashboard with a balanced scorecard containing up to 16 operational KPIs. These KPIs are crucial for monitoring the effectiveness of daily operations and ensuring that the organization is on track to achieve its short-term objectives.

For further clarification on this topic, Figure 2-1 illustrates the four types of Performance Measures, categorizing them in a way that emphasizes their distinct roles. Additionally, Figure 2-2 provides specific examples of each of these four types, enhancing understanding of how KRIs and KPIs can be effectively utilized within an organizational setting. This structured approach not only explains responsibilities at different levels of management but also leads to improved decision-making and enhanced organizational performance.

4 TYPES OF PERFORMANCE MEASURES

Result Indicators	Key Result Indicators	Performance Indicators	Key Performance Indicators
Informs what you have done	Informs how you have done against a Balanced Scorecard perspective or a Critical Success Factor	Informs you what to do	Informs you what to do to improve performance in key areas

Figure 2-1. *Four types of Performance Measures*

EXAMPLES FROM 4 TYPES OF PERFORMANCE MEASURES

Result Indicators

Net Profit on Key Product Line
Hospital Bed Utilization Last week

Key Result Indicators

CSAT
Profit per Customer

Performance Indicators

No. of Sales Calls Organized for next 2 weeks
No. of late deliveries to Key Customers in last 2 weeks

Key Performance Indicators

No. of late flights yesterday
Transaction Completion Rate in a website

Figure 2-2. *Performance Measures examples*

Actual KPIs need to be reported and tracked daily or weekly. Metrics assessed quarterly or annually do not qualify as KPIs. For instance, if customer satisfaction is evaluated only every six months or annually, it cannot serve as an actionable driver. Thus, it is merely a KRI rather than a KPI. A KPI must specify the necessary actions to be taken. Six defining parameters of a KPI are captured in the following Figure 2-3.

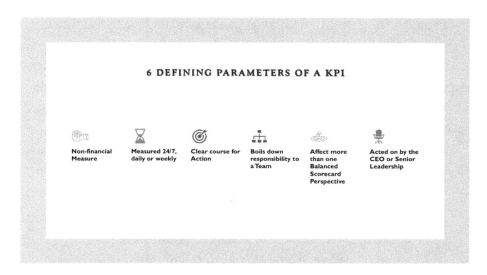

Figure 2-3. *Defining Parameters of a KPI*

Seven steps to develop a KPI are captured in the following Figure 2-4.

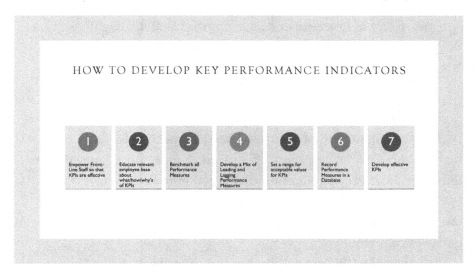

Figure 2-4. *How to develop KPIs*

To lead a "sense-and-respond" organization, managers must have effective sensory tools or "radar screens." Lord King of Wartnaby, who was tasked to turn around British Airways (BA) in the 1980s, concentrated on just one KPI—if a BA plane was delayed. A personal call from Lord King was made to the senior officials at relevant airports if a flight was delayed beyond a certain threshold.

This KPI affected all the balanced scorecard perspectives: financial returns, customer results, internal processes, and learning and growth.

- *Financials*: Delayed flights lead to increased costs due to extra airport fees and accommodation expenses for passengers. Additionally, planes consume more fuel when they have to circle the airport after missing their landing slots due to delays.

- *Customers*: Delays are a key source of customer dissatisfaction.

- *Internal Processes and Learning and Growth*: Flight delays interrupt service schedules, negatively impacting service quality. Moreover, managing customer complaints results in unhappy staff, further lowering morale among key employees.

The "late flight" KPI of BA emphasized the need to focus on recovering the lost time. Cleaners, caterers, ground crew, flight attendants, liaison officers and traffic controllers all work together to save precious seconds. A good KPI has a knock-on effect. Improving flight time, for example, lowers fuel costs, speeds up flight arrivals and departures, and, ultimately, increases profitability.

In retrospect, KRIs are metrics often confused with KPIs. They include:

- Customer satisfaction
- Net profit before tax

- Profitability of customers

- Employee satisfaction

- Return on capital employed

These measures share a common trait: they are the outcomes of various actions, offering a clear indication of whether you are heading in the right direction. However, they do not specify what needs to be done to enhance these results. Consequently, KRIs provide valuable information for the board, meaning those not engaged in day-to-day management.

KRIs typically span a longer time frame than KPIs; they are evaluated on monthly or quarterly cycles rather than daily or weekly, as is the case with KPIs. Differentiating KRIs from other metrics dramatically influences reporting, leading to a division between governance-focused measures and those pertinent to management. This means an organization should have a governance dashboard featuring up to ten high-level KRIs for the board and a balanced scorecard containing up to 20 measures—a blend of KPIs, RIs, and PIs—for day-to-day management.

Between KRIs and true KPIs lie numerous performance and result indicators, which complement the KPIs and are displayed alongside them on scorecards for the organization, as well as for each division, department, and team.

The roughly 80 performance metrics that exist between KRIs and KPIs include performance and result indicators (PIs and RIs). While performance indicators are significant, they are not critical for the business. PIs assist teams in aligning with the organization's strategy. These non-financial indicators complement KPIs and are presented alongside them on the scorecards of each organization, division, department, and team.

Performance indicators below KPIs can include:

- Percentage increase in sales from the top 10% of customers

- Number of employee suggestions implemented in the past 30 days

- Customer complaints from key clients

- Sales calls scheduled for the upcoming week or two

- Late deliveries to important customers

RIs summarize activities, with all financial performance measures being RIs (e.g., daily or weekly sales analysis serves as a useful summary but results from the collective efforts of various teams). However, to grasp what needs to be increased or decreased, it is essential to examine the activities that generated the sales (the outcomes). Result indicators beneath KRIs may encompass:

- Net profit from key product lines

- Sales recorded yesterday

- Customer complaints from major clients

- Hospital bed utilization for the week

Utopian Visions of Performance Measurement Systems vs. Reality

"It is the hallmark of any great truth that its negation is also a great truth"

—Niels Bohr

Crucial insights into business performance often remain hidden. While managers change their performance measures, they often fail to recognize these adjustments as genuine improvements. Therefore, a reality check is essential for those striving to establish the ideal measurement system. In an ideally measured world, managers would create optimal performance measurement systems. The chosen measures would adhere to the following criteria:

- There would be a limited number of measures—possibly three financial and three non-financial metrics. This limitation is vital for simplicity, as an overload of measurements can overwhelm cognitive capacity and obscure information.

- Non-financial metrics should predict future financial performance and act as leading indicators, while financial metrics serve as lagging indicators. Non-financial metrics that do not demonstrate the ability to forecast future performance would be excluded, except when required for compliance purposes.

- These measures should be universally applicable across the organization, allowing aggregation from the bottom to the top and enabling managers to analyze performance comprehensively. They must also facilitate performance comparisons between different units.

- The measurement system should exhibit stability, evolving gradually to ensure that individuals remain aware of long-term goals and consistent behaviour.

- Employees should receive compensation based on both financial and verified leading non-financial performance metrics.

However, it is hard to find performance measures that meet these criteria because such a system may not exist. The reasons are:

First, companies are overwhelmed by metrics, and the issue of having too many becomes increasingly significant. It is common for businesses to track 50 to 60 key financial and non-financial metrics.

Secondly, we have advanced in creating and distributing measures faster than we can pinpoint the select non-financial metrics that truly offer predictive insights into financial results. While some non-financial metrics, such as customer satisfaction, can indeed forecast financial performance when measured correctly, the majority remain unvalidated (Anderson, Fornell, and Mazvancheryl 2004).

Third, identifying non-financial metrics that predict financial outcomes and applying them across the organization is particularly challenging. Although it is somewhat easier to identify financial metrics that do, firms still struggle to align shareholder value metrics from the top down through the organization.

The crux of my argument is that the dissatisfaction managers feel with current measures and their demand for improved measures arises from a profound yet frequently overlooked issue. While it may seem that the problem is solely about measurement, the real solution lies beyond just better performance measures. The measurement challenge exists because a company's overall performance cannot be fully quantified. In the end, company performance directly correlates with future cash flows—"cash flows yet to come"—discounted to present value (Fisher, 1988). By nature, future cash flows cannot be measured; we can only gauge past cash flows (financial performance) and potential indicators of future cash flows (non-financial metrics), as well as proxies like stock prices. All these are imperfect representations—what I categorically label as "second-guess" metrics.

The objective is to pinpoint the best among these second-guess options, sometimes through rigorous analysis and other times through informed intuition. It is essential to recognize that measurement is not the core issue. If it were, managers would be increasingly satisfied as their measures become more precise. Instead, frustration is escalating.

The underlying issue is rooted in our dated understanding of what an organization truly represents and the nature of performance itself. We frequently perceive organizations as enigmatic systems. Funds are injected as investments, a series of unseen activities transpire within the organization's internal mechanisms, and ultimately, products are created for consumers. This process culminates in the generation of key financial documents such as income statements, balance sheets, and market valuations.

Furthermore, the financial outcomes—like income statements, balance sheets, and market valuations—are typically aggregated at the organizational level or categorized into broad segments like various business units. However, the reliance on these aggregate metrics can hide critical variations that exist within different parts of the organization. This blend often results in a misleading portrayal where high-performing segments are merged with those that are underperforming, thereby concealing essential insights and details about the true scale and nature of organizational performance and its various components.

How Can the Firm's Performance Be Made More Transparent?

"I got into the Upanishads to ask questions"

—Niels Bohr

To uncover hidden information about a company and ensure that its performance is fully transparent, we must revisit and deepen our understanding of its fundamental nature and operations. At its core, a company can be viewed as a systematic collection of activities—a series of processes that interact with one another. Each of these activities incurs costs and has the potential to create value for the firm's customers.

When a firm's activities create value for customers, this, in turn, results in increased revenue for the organization. Revenue is the lifeblood of any business, as it reflects customers' willingness to pay for the perceived value of the products or services offered. However, if certain activities fail to deliver that value, customers may choose to withhold their purses, which will negatively impact the firm's financial health.

Consequently, the core components that define a firm can be broken down into a few key elements: the activities it undertakes, the costs associated with these activities, the customers who ultimately decide the value of these activities, and the revenues generated. The interplay between these components is critical, as it highlights the delicate balance between the cost base and the value creation base.

The real challenge firms face is accurately identifying, evaluating, and optimizing specific activities that deliver genuine customer value while also generating revenues that sufficiently exceed their associated costs. At the same time, organizations must seek to expand upon those activities that add value while minimizing or eliminating activities that do not contribute to customer value and instead incur unnecessary costs.

Performance measures are critical tools that enable organizations to assess whether their activities are delivering revenues that surpass their underlying costs and whether they are genuinely delivering value to customers. Understanding and leveraging these performance measures is crucial, and this is the central theme of this section.

While the initial identification of suitable performance measures may appear to be a straightforward endeavor, the actual process of measuring performance and effectively interpreting the resulting data is often far more intricate than it seems. This complexity arises due to a multitude of factors that must be considered, including shifting market dynamics, variations in customer behavior, and the intricacies of internal processes. Each of these elements plays a significant role in shaping the overall business performance landscape.

For instance, market dynamics can change rapidly due to economic fluctuations, competitive pressures, and technological advancements, all of which can impact an organization's performance metrics. Similarly, understanding customer behavior is essential; it involves analyzing purchasing patterns, preferences, and feedback to ensure that customer needs are being met and exceeded. On the internal front, organizations must consider their operational efficiencies, employee performance, and resource allocation, all of which contribute to the overall effectiveness of delivering value.

As we will explore further in this section, this inherent complexity underscores the importance of business performance analysis. By effectively analyzing performance, organizations can navigate these challenges, adapt to changing circumstances, and work toward achieving sustainable success over the long term. Business performance analysis not only aids in identifying areas for improvement but also aligns organizational objectives with customer needs and market realities, thereby fostering a culture of continuous improvement and innovation.

After conducting an in-depth analysis, I have come to the strong conclusion that possessing a fundamental understanding of the firm is not merely advantageous; it is absolutely essential for success in the current business landscape. The core challenge we confront extends beyond the pursuit of improved measures for assessing firm-level performance; instead, it lies in the critical task of accurately pinpointing the specific activities and processes that genuinely create value for customers.

This understanding is paramount because it directly influences our ability to secure revenues that significantly surpass costs because customers pay when companies deliver value. My conclusion has emerged from grappling with various anomalies—situations and concepts that starkly contradict conventional wisdom or established norms. These discrepancies highlight the complexities of business operations and the necessity for a nuanced approach to identifying what drives true value within organizations. By doing so, we can better align firm strategies with customer needs and enhance the firm's overall effectiveness in the marketplace.

We simply cannot afford to overlook the fact that true performance in a business context is not merely about executing tasks but about understanding which activities drive value creation. This realization is imperative if we are to achieve sustainable profitability and maintain a competitive edge. Therefore, we must shift our focus from generic performance measures to the performance measures of specific activities that contribute significantly to a firm's success in the marketplace. This change in perspective is not just necessary; it is crucial for ensuring that organizations are measured by the impact they create rather than by superficial metrics that fail to capture their true performance.

Another striking anomaly is that the various performance measures used by firms often exhibit little or no correlation with each other. This inconsistency raises critical questions about the adequacy and reliability of the measurement systems currently employed by organizations to evaluate success and efficiency.

The underlying issue prompts us to consider why organizations—especially those committed to achieving high-performance outcomes—would continue to rely on such ineffective measurement practices. This concern becomes even more significant when we consider that many employees' compensation packages are directly tied to these performance assessments. Relying on metrics that may not accurately reflect individual contributions poses serious implications for fairness and motivation in the workplace.

The Quest to Identify the Revenue Drivers: The Riveting Story of Activity-Based Revenue

The pursuit of performance and process transparency leads us to identify the key revenue drivers of an organization. In that context, I would firmly assert that the concept of activity-based costing (ABC) must be reimagined to effectively identify revenue drivers, drawing on the pivotal research conducted by Cooper and Kaplan in 1992. This innovative inversion of ABC is known as activity-based revenue (ABR), and it offers a strategic framework that organizations cannot afford to overlook. ABR is not just a theoretical construct; its grounding in the established principles of ABC makes it a practical and accessible tool for firms striving to enhance their performance.

What sets ABR apart is its powerful capacity to streamline a firm's activities, along with the associated costs, customer relationships, and revenue streams. Embracing reductionism—a time-honored principle in science—this approach simplifies complex organizational operations into essential components, leading to greater clarity and control. It is high time we applied these reductionist principles to firm management and, specifically, to performance measurement.

The existing framework for performance measurement is inherently problematic due to its firm-centric perspective. This approach treats the firm as an isolated entity, concentrating on evaluating both financial and non-financial performance metrics strictly at the organizational level.

The process typically begins by examining the firm's financial outcomes—profit margins, revenue growth, and return on investment—seeking to discern how various operational processes influence these results. However, this method often overlooks the broader context in which the firm operates, including the impact of external stakeholders, market dynamics, and inter-firm relationships.

The ultimate goal of this firm-level analysis is to identify appropriate non-financial measures that can effectively assess the firm's overall performance. These measures can include aspects such as employee satisfaction, customer loyalty, and innovation capabilities. Yet, the firm-centric viewpoint limits the understanding of how interdependencies with external factors might also contribute to the firm's success or failures, thereby undermining the holistic evaluation that is needed in today's "Sense-and-Respond" business environments.

The quest for effective non-financial performance metrics is riddled with obstacles, as these indicators are often difficult to establish and lead to ongoing disputes among managers over their relevance and accuracy. This dissatisfaction serves as a clear signal that we need a paradigm shift. To truly enhance our understanding and measurement of organizational performance, it is imperative we move beyond the limitations of a firm-centric approach and embrace a broader perspective that aligns with the intricacies of revenue generation and performance enhancement.

As a result, a more comprehensive performance measurement framework is necessary—one that acknowledges and integrates the intricacies of both internal processes and external influences, providing a well-rounded understanding of what drives performance in a modern firm.

Activity-centric performance measurement is a comprehensive framework that dissects an organization into its fundamental activities, enabling a thorough analysis of the costs and revenues linked to each individual operation. This approach is better than traditional firm-centric measurement techniques, which typically assess the organization's overall performance as a single entity without delving into the intricacies of its various functions. By focusing on specific activities, this method allows management to understand the unique contribution of each process to the organization's profitability and overall financial health.

By conducting a thorough and detailed examination of their operations, businesses can pinpoint which specific activities deliver the highest levels of efficiency, generate the largest revenue streams, or result in the greatest expenses. This process involves meticulously quantifying performance across various functions and departments at a granular level. By doing so, organizations empower themselves to make well-informed decisions regarding the allocation of resources, which processes need improvement, and how to effectively align their strategic planning with operational realities.

Furthermore, this detailed analysis promotes a culture of accountability within the organization. When individual departments or teams have clear visibility into how their specific actions and decisions directly influence the company's financial health and overall success, they become more motivated to optimize their performance. This heightened awareness fosters a sense of responsibility and ownership over outcomes, encouraging teams to strive for continuous improvement.

Ultimately, adopting an activity-centric approach to performance measurement equips organizational leaders with incisive insights. These insights facilitate informed decision-making that drives operational excellence and strengthens competitive advantage. By understanding which activities contribute most significantly to their goals, organizations can streamline processes, enhance productivity, and better position themselves in the marketplace.

In the Activity-Based Revenue (ABR) framework, organizations can precisely measure the costs associated with various activities. This provides valuable insights into how much financial resources each specific activity consumes, allowing for a thorough analysis of operational efficiency and cost management.

When examining the revenue side of operations, it's important to recognize that directly allocating revenue to specific activities can often be more intricate and may introduce certain challenges. The complexity arises from the need to accurately trace revenue to particular activities, especially when multiple initiatives or services intersect in generating income. However, overcoming these challenges is entirely achievable through the implementation of indirect methods that provide reliable revenue metrics.

To effectively accomplish this, organizations should focus on gathering and analyzing a broad spectrum of data related to customer interactions. This data collection should encompass various aspects, including customer purchase behaviors, engagement levels with different services, and the performance measures of individual activities. By systematically tracking how different activities function and the associated revenue they produce, companies can develop a clearer picture of their financial landscape.

For instance, sophisticated tracking methodologies such as multi-touch attribution can help in understanding the extent to which each activity contributes to overall revenue, even when precise direct allocations are impractical. This approach could involve using analytics tools, such as Google Analytics, that measure customer journeys across multiple touchpoints, allowing businesses to assess how marketing campaigns, promotional offers, or product developments influence purchasing decisions.

Moreover, this holistic view enables organizations to make well-informed strategic decisions. By having a nuanced understanding of both the costs associated with various activities and the revenue they generate, businesses can optimize resource allocation, refine their marketing strategies, and identify areas for potential growth. Ultimately, adopting this comprehensive understanding of revenue generation encourages a more effective and informed approach to managing business activities, aligning objectives with financial performance goals.

The Power of Activity-Centric Performance Measurement: Knowing Where the Value Is Created or Lost

The principal distinction between firm-centric and activity-centric performance measurement is unequivocal: firm-centric measurement focuses on the organization in its entirety, while activity-centric measurement focuses on individual activities. This concentrated analysis empowers senior management to identify exactly where value is created or lost. By utilizing this approach, businesses can make decisive and informed choices regarding resource allocation and strategic direction, driving enhanced performance and profitability.

Moreover, the distinctions between firm-centric and activity-centric performance measurement have profound implications for the quality and reliability of performance measurement systems in organizations. Firm-centric performance measurement attempts to capture every aspect of a firm's operations, resulting in a vast array of non-financial metrics that often lack clarity and relevance to actual performance. This scattergun approach creates significant uncertainty regarding the insights these measures provide. Without rigorous statistical testing—which frequently proves inconclusive—organizations cannot confidently assert the effectiveness of these metrics.

In contrast, activity-centric performance measurement emerges as a notably more precise and effective strategy for evaluating organizational performance and can act like a sniper. This approach requires the development of a comprehensive dictionary that details each activity carried out by the firm. Such a dictionary not only lists these activities but also provides clear definitions and classifications that capture the nuances of each task.

Also, a thorough assessment of both the costs incurred and revenues generated by every identified activity is imperative. This involves collecting data and analyzing various financial metrics associated with

33

each task, ensuring a complete understanding of their economic impact. While the implementation of this process can be resource-intensive and demand significant effort across various departments, the benefits of this investment are undeniable.

The structured nature of activity-centric performance measurement offers a significant advantage: it brings rigour, clarity, and transparency to the financial outcomes connected to individual activities. By aligning costs and revenues with specific tasks, organizations can identify which activities are driving value and which are hindering profitability. This level of insight enables more informed decision-making and strategic planning, ultimately allowing firms to optimize their operations and enhance overall financial performance.

This performance measurement approach allows organizations to make astute, informed decisions by establishing direct links between revenues and costs associated with specific activities. This method highlights how specific activities directly drive profitability which should be the center of gravity for all analysis of a firm's business performance. Firms must recognize that this approach delivers improved operational effectiveness and increased business process transparency.

By focusing on the activities that have the most profound impact on their bottom line, businesses can effectively navigate industry complexities and ensure they achieve sustained financial success. The time to commit to this activity-centric performance measurement approach is now.

Summary

Many firms emphasize the importance of performance. But a common feeling of dissatisfaction persists regarding the performance measurement systems used. Many organizations—possibly most—view their performance frameworks as insufficient. A key reason for this dissatisfaction is the lack of robust non-financial indicators, including customer service quality, research and development success, initial product quality, and ongoing employee development.

Going back to the fundamentals, performance measures come in four different varieties:

1. Result Indicators (RI)

2. Key Result Indicators (KRI)

3. Performance Indicators (PI)

4. Key Performance Indicators (KPI)

Key Performance Indicators (KPIs) are essential tools for operating managers. They provide them with advance warning signals that can indicate potential challenges or problems that may arise in the future. These signals are crucial as they help managers understand which proactive actions need to be taken to mitigate risks and enhance overall performance. It is important to differentiate between leading performance measures, which are represented by KPIs, and lagging performance measures, which are captured by Key Result Indicators (KRIs). KPIs focus on predictive metrics that can drive performance improvements, while KRIs reflect outcomes that have already occurred.

Despite using the right performance measures, important insights into business performance often go unnoticed. While managers alter their performance measures, they frequently overlook these changes as true improvements. A reality check is therefore vital for those aiming to develop the perfect measurement system. In an ideally measured world, managers would craft optimal performance measurement systems.

But, it is essential to recognize that measurement is not the core issue. If it were, managers would be increasingly satisfied as their measures become more precise. Instead, frustration is escalating. The underlying issue is rooted in our dated understanding of what an organization truly represents and the nature of performance itself. We frequently perceive organizations as enigmatic systems. Funds are injected as investments, a series of unseen activities transpire within the organization's internal mechanisms, and ultimately, products are created for consumers. This process culminates in the generation of key financial documents such as income statements, balance sheets, and market valuations.

Furthermore, the financial outcomes—like income statements, balance sheets, and market valuations—are typically aggregated at the organizational level or categorized into broad segments like various business units. However, the reliance on these aggregate metrics can hide critical variations that exist within different parts of the organization. This blend often results in a misleading portrayal where high-performing segments are merged with those that are underperforming, thereby concealing essential insights and details about the true scale and nature of organizational performance and its various components. The only way to reveal the essential insights is to change course—from firm-centric performance measurement to activity-centric performance measurement practices.

CHAPTER 3

Setting Up Performance Frameworks and Creating Blueprints for Success

Setting up Performance Frameworks are pivotal to accomplishing stellar business performance. However, implementing effective performance frameworks, like the Balanced Scorecard, does not guarantee better organizational performance, as strategy execution is a big anathema for managers. Why is that true? A common issue is incorrect assumptions about the validity of a firm's business model, which plagues most organizations.

While the intuition of the senior leadership is priceless, it must be complemented by performance measurement data to provide critical insights. Misalignment between operational processes and strategic goals often leads to futile implementation. The importance of establishing specific processes and capabilities necessary for strategy execution is of paramount importance.

© Suvradeep Bhattacharjee 2025
S. Bhattacharjee, *Path to Stellar Business Performance Analysis*,
https://doi.org/10.1007/979-8-8688-1501-0_3

To bridge the gap of this misalignment between strategy and operations, organizations should identify the processes that support strategic initiatives and assess the capabilities, that is, skills, tools, and resources required. In this pursuit for stellar strategy execution, performance measurement plays a crucial role by identifying which business processes are pivotal for executing the strategy and which business processes drive competitive advantage. This endeavor will allow for better resource allocation toward sustainable growth and innovation.

Types of Performance Frameworks

Is it not strange that desire should so many years outlive performance?

—William Shakespeare

Performance measures define the Performance Frameworks which inherit them, making the selection of these measures a critical aspect of developing effective performance frameworks. In other words, the specific characteristics and efficacy of performance frameworks are largely determined by the types of measures employed to evaluate performances.

A pioneering study by Fitzgerald et al. in 1991 delved into the intricacies of performance measurement within service industries. It classified performance measures into two primary categories.

The first category captures performance outcomes, which focus on the end results of key activities. These measures include indicators such as competitiveness in the market and overall financial performance, allowing organizations to measure how well they are achieving their strategic goals and accomplishing their missions.

The second category captures the key drivers of those outcomes. This includes measures that interrogate various factors pivotal to organizational performance, such as quality of service delivery, flexibility to adapt to changing market conditions, resource efficiency in operations, and the capacity for innovation. By capturing these underlying factors, organizations will gain insights into their operational processes and identify areas for improvement that could lead to better internal performance.

In summary, the interplay between performance measures and frameworks is crucial. It highly influences how organizations measure success and drive strategic decision-making processes.

The primary benefit of embracing the results–determinants framework is its emphasis on causality. This framework emphasizes that the business outcomes we get today are significantly influenced by past actions. By acknowledging this cause-and-effect relationship, captured in Figure 3-1, we can get deeper insights into how past decisions and actions impact current performance.

This causal performance framework aims to implement a range of performance measurement systems. These performance measurement systems are designed to identify the key performance drivers that are essential for achieving the desired performance outcomes. By meticulously analyzing these drivers, organizations can better identify which levers they need to pull to enhance their performance effectively. Ultimately, this causal approach brings clarity about how various performance drivers interact with desired performance outcomes, enabling better decisions and sound strategic planning required for sustainable success.

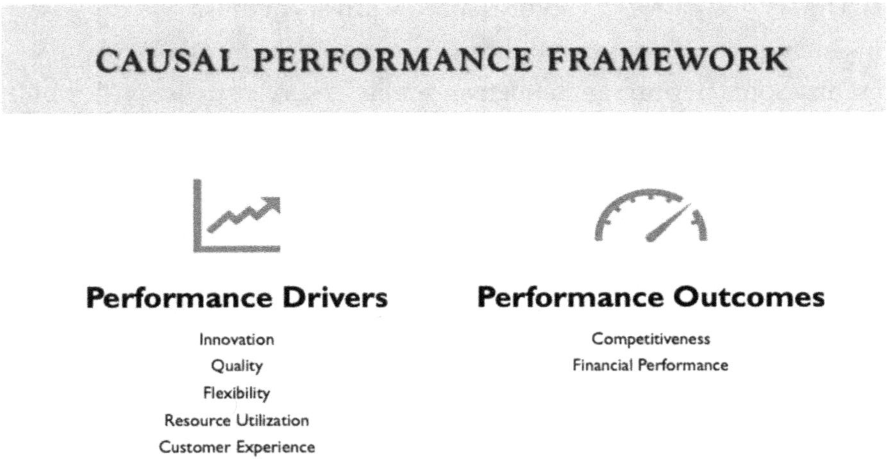

CAUSAL PERFORMANCE FRAMEWORK

Performance Drivers

Innovation
Quality
Flexibility
Resource Utilization
Customer Experience

Performance Outcomes

Competitiveness
Financial Performance

Figure 3-1. *The Causal Performance Framework*

This Causal Performance Framework paved the way for Brown's 1996 introduction of the "Performance Framework with a Firm-Level View." Brown's framework builds upon the idea of establishing connections between key performance measures through a systematic understanding of cause-and-effect relationships at different stages of organizational life cycle. It expands the scope of causal performance analysis into a comprehensive macro process model that focuses specifically on the functioning of a firm.

Although this framework may present a simplified view, it effectively categorizes various performance measures associated with each stage of a firm's activities, that is, input, process, output, and goal. This classification allows managers to gain incisive insights into the intricate dynamics of how their performance measures interact with each other. These insights are illustrated in the accompanying Figure 3-2, which represents the interdependencies of the different stages and their respective performance measures within the context of a firm's operations.

Brown delineates four distinct yet interconnected stages within a business process: input, process, output, and goal in his framework. Each of these stages contains unique performance measures that are critical for evaluating the overall efficacy of a firm's operations. The framework operates under the assumption of a linear relationship where each preceding stage serves as a building block for the subsequent stage. In other words, the quality and characteristics of inputs directly determine the processes that transform these inputs, which in turn decide the outputs ultimately accomplished, leading toward the firm's overarching goals.

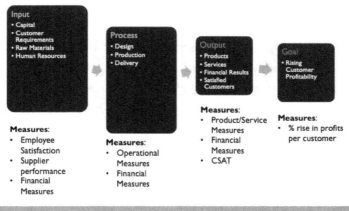

Figure 3-2. *The Performance Framework with a Firm-Level View*

Balanced Scorecards

"Life is like riding a bicycle. To keep your balance, you must keep moving."

—Albert Einstein

The Balanced Scorecard, arguably the most popular performance framework developed by Robert Kaplan and David Norton in the early 1990s, has built its reputation as the most established approach for assessing organizational performance. First introduced in 1992 and later refined in 1996, the Balanced Scorecard encompasses four distinct perspectives that provide a holistic view of a company's performance: financial returns, customer results, internal processes, and learning and growth.

The Learning and Growth perspective serves as a crucial enabler for the other three perspectives—financial, customer, and internal processes. This perspective is made of three key areas of capital:

1. *Human Capital*: This refers to the knowledge, skills, and abilities of an organization's workforce. Investing in training, development, and employee well-being fosters a more competent and motivated team that drives innovation and improves performance.

2. *Information Capital*: This encompasses the systems, technologies, and data that support decision-making and strategic planning. By leveraging advanced information management and analytics, organizations can gain insights that lead to better results and bigger competitive advantages.

3. *Organizational Capital*: This includes the culture, structure, and processes that shape an organization's operations. Establishing a strong organizational framework facilitates collaboration, knowledge sharing, and adaptability, enabling the organization to respond in an agile and effective way to shifting environments.

Together, these three elements of the Learning and Growth perspective empower the other three perspectives—financial returns, customer results, and internal processes. The financial perspective focuses on the tangible results of an organization's operations, measuring profitability, revenue growth, and cost management. The customer perspective accentuates customer satisfaction and retention, analyzing metrics such as customer loyalty, market share, and the effectiveness of customer service initiatives. The internal processes perspective looks at the internal operations that contribute to the company's success, evaluating efficiency, quality, and innovation in key processes. Finally, the learning and growth perspective addresses the importance of organizational growth by gauging the development of employee skills, knowledge acquisition, and the effectiveness of training programs.

In essence, an essential principle of the Balanced Scorecard is its assertion that organizations should place equal weightage on financial performance and the underlying drivers of that performance—customer results and internal processes. Moreover, it emphasizes the significance of continuous learning and development as a means to sustain competitive advantage and secure long-term success.

The Balanced Scorecard is quite similar to other performance frameworks, particularly those that employ causal relationships and focus on macro-level models. But, Balanced Scorecards distinguishes itself by its explicit alignment with the organization's strategy. This strategic link is central, as it ensures that the performance measures not only evaluate outcomes but also connect to the overarching strategy of the firm.

To illustrate this concept of linking strategy to performance measures, I employed the metaphor of a tree in Figure 3-3. This metaphor effectively captures the intricate internal dynamics of a company and symbolizes how various elements of performance interconnect to support the overall strategic vision.

Figure 3-3. The Tree of Balanced Scorecard

The balanced scorecard can only be effective when an organization connects its performance measures to its overarching business strategy. This alignment is crucial and can be accomplished by thoroughly identifying and understanding the key drivers that influence organizational performance, a concept emphasized by Kaplan and Norton in their research from 1996. These drivers are captured in the Causal Performance Framework, illustrated in Figure 3-1. By mapping out these relationships, organizations can ensure that their performance measures are not isolated metrics but rather integral components that support and reflect their strategic objectives. This rounded approach enables organizations to create a more focused and comprehensive roadmap for achieving their goals and enhancing overall business performance.

Performance measures function as essential gauges that provide insight into whether the organization is successfully navigating toward its strategic goals. They offer prized feedback on the progress being made, helping to assess whether the organization is on the right path, moving at an appropriate pace, and maintaining sufficient resources— metaphorically referred to as fuel—to reach its ultimate objectives.

By integrating these performance measures into the balanced
scorecard framework, firms can track their current performance, identify
areas for improvement, ensure strategic alignment across all levels,
curate a culture of accountability, and maintain continuous growth.
This performance framework empowers organizations to translate their
strategic vision into actionable plans, thus enhancing their chances of
achieving longer-term success.

The Balanced Scorecard executes organizational strategy into action
through four essential components:

> *Objectives*: These clearly defined goals align with
> your organization's vision, directing efforts toward
> meaningful outcomes.

> *Measures*: These indicators provide incisive
> insights into performance, allowing you to see
> how effectively you are progressing toward your
> objectives.

> *Targets*: By establishing specific performance
> benchmarks, targets drive accountability and
> motivate teams to achieve exceptional results within
> set timelines.

> *Strategic Initiatives*: These concrete action plans
> outline the steps necessary to transform objectives
> into reality, ensuring that resources are effectively
> deployed to maximize impact.

At its very core, the Balanced Scorecard is designed for translation. It
takes abstract concepts such as the firm's mission, vision, and strategic
goals and translates them into concrete performance objectives and
measurable outcomes. These performance objectives are aligned with
four distinct perspectives of the Scorecard: Financial, Customer, Internal
Processes, and Learning and growth.

By defining specific targets for each measure, the Balanced Scorecard injects vitality into these performance measures, allowing organizations to track progress meaningfully. Furthermore, strategic initiatives are deployed to bridge the performance gap between current results and the desired outcomes outlined in the vision. These initiatives are often geared toward fostering behavioral changes within the organization, ensuring that every level of the workforce is engaged in the journey toward achieving the company's overarching goals.

In essence, the Balanced Scorecard provides a comprehensive performance framework for aiding a deeper understanding of organizational dynamics, aligning activities with the vision and strategy, and driving performance improvement across various business areas.

One significant advantage of implementing the Balanced Scorecard is its ability to encapsulate the firm's strategic intent in a manner that is easily understood by all team members. This process begins with a clear articulation of the mission, which serves as the foundation for all subsequent translation efforts. A well-crafted Balanced Scorecard not only captures this mission but also translates it into specific objectives depicted on the strategy map. Furthermore, the measures tracked on the Scorecard are designed to closely reflect these objectives, ensuring a cohesive relationship between the firm's strategic goals and the performance measures employed.

Despite the positives, the balanced scorecard has several shortcomings that can undermine its effectiveness. One such serious shortcoming is the lack of a competitive dimension. Understanding a firm's performance relative to its competitors is fundamental for a rigorous assessment of strategy execution. Without the competitive perspective, firms will miss critical insights that inform benchmarking and strategic positioning within their industry.

Additionally, the balanced scorecard fails to include perspectives on four vital variables that are essential (as highlighted by experts such as Maisel, 1992; Ewing and Lundahl, 1996; Lingle and Schiemann, 1996; and Brown, 1996). These variables are:

1. *Employee Satisfaction*: The absence of employee satisfaction could lead to a lack of innovation and engagement.

2. *Supplier Performance*: Without measuring supplier performance, companies risk disruptions and inefficiencies in their supply chains.

3. *Product/Service Quality*: Neglecting this dimension may result in diminishing product offerings that do not meet evolving customer expectations.

4. *Environmental and Community Considerations*: Firms can no longer afford to overlook their environmental impact and community role. Failure to focus on this aspect will result in reputational damage and increased regulatory scrutiny.

If these five perspectives are excluded, the balanced scorecard will limit an organization's ability to fully understand and enhance its strategic performance.

Performance Measurement, Performance Analysis, and Strategy Execution

Will implementing effective Performance Frameworks, such as the Balanced Scorecard, lead us to the proverbial "promised land" of enhanced organizational performance? While identifying the firm's strategy and assigning appropriate performance measures is certainly a crucial step, the answer is a resounding no. In fact, research indicates that a significant majority of managers struggle to execute their organizations' strategies successfully.

One primary reason for this failure is faulty assumptions about which strategies really drive improved business performance. When these assumptions are incorrect, the anticipated benefits and outcomes will not materialize, leading to missed opportunities and potential decline. It is absolutely critical to evaluate whether a firm's business model holds up to scrutiny, as its validity is central to the success of any strategy execution.

Although senior leadership's intuition and insights are invaluable, they cannot be relied upon exclusively. This is where performance measurement data comes into play. By leveraging this data and conducting a thorough analysis, organizations can gain critical insights that not only aid in decision-making but also significantly bolster the evaluation of their business model's validity. In essence, an astute blend of leadership intuition and data-driven insights creates a stronger base for determining the efficacy of a firm strategy and improves the chances of achieving the desired outcomes.

The second significant reason organizations fail to implement their strategies effectively is the misalignment between their operational processes and overarching strategic goals. Even in cases where processes are aligned with company strategy, the capabilities required to execute these processes successfully are frequently lacking.

To bridge the gap that exists between strategy formulation and execution, it is crucial to reflect on two fundamental questions:

1. What specific processes must be established to facilitate the successful execution of the organization's strategies?

    a. This involves identifying the critical tasks, workflows, and operational frameworks that need to be developed to support strategic initiatives. It requires a thorough understanding of how these processes can translate strategic visions into actionable steps.

2. What capabilities are required to effectively operate
    these processes?

    a. This encompasses not only the skills and expertise
        of the workforce but also the tools, technologies,
        and resources needed to perform the tasks at hand.
        It is essential to assess whether the organization
        possesses the right talent and systems in place to
        enable these processes to function optimally.

Addressing these questions can help organizations create a more
coherent alignment between their strategies and operations, eventually
increasing the chance of successful implementation.

Performance measurement is an excellent tool to address these two
questions. Performance measurement tools systematically quantify the
efficiency and effectiveness of key business processes. Based on the
implementation of these measurement techniques, we can conduct
rigorous performance analyses to deliver incisive insights.

These incisive insights will help identify specific business processes
and capabilities that help build a competitive advantage for the firm.
Such processes and underlying capabilities are aligned with the firm's
strategy. These processes usually generate real value and foster innovation.
On the other hand, performance measurement tools also reveal those
processes and capabilities that simply require routine maintenance, as
those processes do not contribute significantly to competitive success.
This nuanced understanding enables the firm to allocate resources more
effectively and prioritize which business processes to develop first, which
will secure market leadership.

Measurement of Input, Process, and Output of a Firm

When designing measurement processes, it is crucial to adopt the customer's perspective. Customers' expectations often emphasize three key factors: speed, accuracy, and cost-effectiveness. Understanding these priorities is essential for creating processes that truly meet customer needs.

A typical process consists of several distinct stages, and if the final output is flawed—whether incorrect, costly, or delivered later than promised—it can be challenging to pinpoint the specific components within the process that contributed to these issues. This ambiguity raises an important question: How can one identify which elements require improvement?

In practice, it is all too easy to track numerous metrics without gaining meaningful insights, which ultimately defeats the purpose of measurement. Therefore, it is paramount to establish process owners. These individuals play a critical role in ensuring that the measurement framework is effective and focused. Process Owners ensure that measurement practices deliver incisive insights and drive continual improvement that is aligned with customer expectations.

Process owners are responsible for making several key decisions, including

1. *Identifying Important Measures*: They determine which performance measures are really significant in evaluating the success of the process from the customer's standpoint. Metrics are building blocks of Performance Measures.

2. *Selecting Applicable Metrics*: They choose the appropriate metrics that align with the essential measures, ensuring relevance and facilitating actionable insights.

3. *Determining Measurement Frequency*: Process owners decide how often to measure these identified metrics to provide timely feedback and support ongoing improvements.

4. *Assigning Measurement Responsibilities*: Finally, Process Owners establish who within the organization will be responsible for gathering and reporting these metrics, ensuring accountability and clarity in the measurement process.

Understanding how business processes are organized is central to developing the know-how of how performance frameworks benefit an organization. Business processes operate on a foundation of capabilities essential for a firm's overall functioning. Capabilities are built by a combination of a company's workforce, methodologies, technological resources, and infrastructural components. Together, these elements form a framework that empowers the organization to deliver value to its stakeholders.

A business process is characterized by its unique underlying components and capabilities that drive that process. These process components and underlying capabilities set one business process apart from other business processes within the organization. To ensure that these processes remain effective and competitive, measurement processes should concentrate on the critical underlying elements that make them distinct. This focus is crucial for assessing current performance and for anticipating future needs and developments, ensuring that the organization can adapt and thrive in a constantly evolving landscape. Once these critical elements are prioritized over others, firms can increase their ability to create and sustain value over time.

Competitive benchmarking is another important tool in a Performance Analyst's toolkit. By examining key performance indicators and best practices within the industry, firms can identify specific areas where they can excel and where there is room for improvement. To gauge the disparity between a firm and its competitors in critical business processes and capabilities, competitive benchmarks play a vital role. These benchmarks provide a quantitative and qualitative analysis of performance, efficiency, and market positioning.

Also, the firm's competitors navigate similar stakeholder landscapes, each striving to create unique value propositions for their respective stakeholders. This benchmarking exercise highlights the gaps between firms offering valuable insights into innovative strategies that others are employing. By better understanding the competitive landscape, firms can make informed decisions, adopt new practices, and enhance their own value creation for stakeholders. Finally, this detailed benchmarking analysis often leads to improved competitive positioning and operational excellence.

Figure 3-4 captures examples of performance measures across a firm's input, process, and output stages.

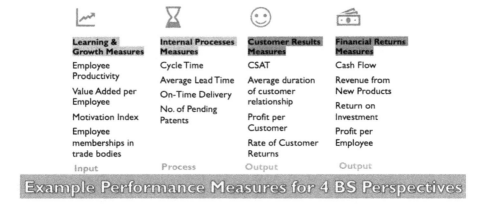

Figure 3-4. Example Performance Measures for 4 BS Perspectives

Devolution of Performance Planning to Frontline Management Is the Way Forward

The rise of "Sense-and-Respond" organizations marks a significant shift in how businesses approach performance planning and performance management. These organizations prioritize adaptability and responsiveness over traditional centralized performance planning systems, which rely on rigid plans, fixed targets, and allocated resources. Such centralized systems were crafted for a more stable "Make-and-Sell" trading environment, which is rapidly becoming obsolete.

In the past, companies would often engage in lengthy negotiations to establish annual goals and resource allocations, believing this structure would provide clarity and direction. However, the changing landscape of business—characterized by rapid technological advancements, shifting consumer demands, and unpredictable market conditions—has rendered these approaches ineffective. As a result, organizations that can quickly sense changes in their environment and respond flexibly are more likely to thrive in today's dynamic marketplace, leading to the decline of outdated centralized performance planning methods.

The legacy of the traditional "Make-and-Sell" business environment has ingrained certain outdated habits that persist in the contemporary "Sense-and-Respond" landscape. Despite the rapid evolution of market dynamics, many organizations dedicate substantial resources to continually aligning and realigning their strategies, structures, and systems. This framework alignment effort is crucial for them to remain competitive in a fast-paced and ever-changing business ecosystem.

As companies strive to shed these outdated frameworks, the struggle to innovate and update practices impacts not only overall efficiency but also employee morale and engagement. In essence, the remnants of the old system create a barrier to embracing the flexibility and responsiveness required in today's business context, making it imperative for organizations to evolve their management approaches to foster resilience and adaptability among their workforces.

In recent years, a significant shift has occurred among pioneering organizations as they transition from a traditional "make-and-sell" model to a more adaptive "sense-and-respond" approach to management. The "make-and-sell" model, rooted in the industrial age, focuses primarily on transactional relationships, emphasizing the importance of tangible capital assets and the efficiencies of mass production. This model is characterized by the pursuit of economies of scale and relies heavily on product margins. Companies operating under this paradigm often prioritize output over input, aiming to maximize profitability through standardized products and large production runs.

Conversely, today's "sense-and-respond" model represents a fundamental shift in thinking, reflecting the realities of the information age. This approach emphasizes the importance of understanding and responding to customer needs and preferences in real time. It fosters deep client relationships and values intellectual assets, enabling organizations to innovate and adapt quickly. Rather than mass production, this model promotes mass customization, allowing businesses to tailor their offerings to individual customer requirements. Furthermore, it leverages economies of scope, focusing on the diversity and complexity of products and services rather than just the volume produced. Ultimately, the sense-and-respond approach is centered on value creation, where companies strive not only to meet market demands but to anticipate them and deliver exceptional customer experiences.

Apple serves as a prime example of a sense-and-respond organization, showcasing how modern businesses can adapt to consumer needs in real time. Unlike traditional companies that rely on a "push" system—where products are developed and pushed through predefined processes to achieve certain sales metrics—Apple adopts a "pull" strategy that places the customer at the forefront of its operations. In this model, customer orders and preferences directly inform the development and refinement of products and services.

One of the key characteristics of sense-and-respond organizations is their rejection of fixed targets and inflexible annual planning. In contrast to conventional approaches that often create rigid barriers to innovation and responsiveness, Apple thrives in an environment that embraces agility and adaptability. Without the constraints of predetermined goals, teams at Apple can pivot quickly in response to market feedback or changes in consumer demand. This flexibility allows the organization to remain attuned to customer needs, driving both employee engagement and the overall effectiveness of its operational processes. As a result, organizations that wish to emulate Apple's success must adopt similar principles that prioritize responsiveness over rigid planning.

Leading firms that excel in sense-and-respond strategies empower their frontline managers with the tools and information necessary to make timely and well-informed decisions. By providing access to comprehensive data analytics, these organizations enable division managers to identify emerging trends, recognize patterns in consumer behavior, and anticipate disruptive market changes long before their competitors catch on. This proactive approach allows them to make strategic decisions about product development and market expansion significantly ahead of time, giving them a competitive edge.

Furthermore, these forward-thinking firms encourage their senior leadership teams to continuously question the validity of their existing business models. This culture of inquiry fosters innovation and adaptability, ensuring that the company remains responsive to shifting market conditions and consumer demands.

Most importantly, these organizations establish robust conduits for knowledge sharing across all levels of the firm. By facilitating open communication and collaboration, they ensure that insights and best practices are disseminated quickly. This agility allows for swift adjustments to strategies and operations, enabling the firm to address potential challenges proactively before they escalate into major issues. In essence, businesses that adopt these practices create a resilient framework that promotes both informed decision-making and rapid response capabilities.

Performance Framework Examples from the UK Government

The UK Government has been using Performance Frameworks across its various departments. Table 3-1 capture the intended outcomes and performance metrics for the Department of Health and Social Care, Department of Education, and Home Office:

*Table 3-1. Performance Framework Example from UK Department of
Health and Social Care*

UK Government Department	Provisional Outcomes (selected)	Provisional Performance Metrics (selected)
Department of Health and Social Care	Improve healthcare outcomes for people by providing high quality and sustainable care at the right time at the right place.	Treatable mortality rate (age-standardized rate per 100,000 population)
		Number of appointments in general practice
		Patient experience of general practice
		Percentage of cancer diagnoses at an early stage (stages 1 and 2)
		One-year cancer survival rate (per cent)
		Number of people accessing Improving Access to Psychological Therapies (IAPT) services
		Number of children and young people accessing NHS funded mental health services
		Percentage of births resulting in stillbirth or neonatal death
		Percentage of patients waiting more than 52 weeks for consultant-led treatment
		A&E performance measure
		Number of new hospitals under construction
		NHS productivity growth rate (per cent)

(continued)

Table 3-1. (*continued*)

UK Government Department	Provisional Outcomes (selected)	Provisional Performance Metrics (selected)
	Improve healthcare outcomes through a supported workforce fit for the future	Number of registered nurses employed by the NHS
		Number of doctors in general practice
		Number of additional primary care professionals in general practice (excluding doctors and nurses)
		Sickness absence rate (per cent)
		Staff engagement rate
		Percentage of staff who say they have personally experienced harassment, bullying or abuse at work from: (a) managers, (b) other colleagues, (c) patients/service users, their relatives or other members of the public in the last 12 months
	Improve and protect the public's health while reducing health inequalities	Disability-free life expectancy at birth— female and male
		Gap in disability free life expectancy at birth (slope index of inequality)—female and male
		Smoking prevalence in adults (per cent)
		Under 75 mortality rate from cardiovascular diseases considered preventable (per 100,000 population)

(*continued*)

Table 3-1. (*continued*)

UK Government Department	Provisional Outcomes (selected)	Provisional Performance Metrics (selected)
		Obesity prevalence—childhood and adult (per cent)
		Total energy and nutrient intakes (including total energy, sugar, fat, salt)
		Percentage of children and adults who are physically active (defined by the Chief Medical Officer's recommendations for physical activity)
	Improve social care outcomes through an affordable, high quality and sustainable adult social care system	Percentage Care Quality Commission locations with an overall rating of outstanding or good
		Social care-related quality of life (score out of 12)
		Carer reported quality of life (score out of 12)
		Percentage of people who use social care services who say that those services have made them feel safe and secure
		Staff turnover rate for directly employed staff working in the adult social care sector (per cent)
		Vacancy rate in adult social care sector (per cent)

Summary

This chapter discusses the importance of performance measures in shaping performance frameworks, underlining that the choice of measures is essential for effective performance management. It categorizes performance measures into two groups:

1. *Outcome-Related Measures*: These focus on the results of performance activities, such as market competitiveness and financial success.

2. *Key Drivers of Outcomes*: This includes measures related to service quality, operational flexibility, resource efficiency, and capacity for innovation.

The results–determinants framework emphasizes understanding the causality between past actions and current business outcomes. By assessing critical performance drivers, organizations can improve their performance and make informed strategic decisions for sustainable success.

The "Crown Jewel" of performance frameworks, The Balanced Scorecard, developed by Robert Kaplan and David Norton in the early 1990s, assesses organizational performance through four interrelated perspectives: financial, customer, internal processes, and learning and growth.

The Learning and Growth perspective is foundational and consists of three key areas:

1. *Human Capital*: Focuses on workforce knowledge and skills, emphasizing training and employee well-being.

2. *Information Capital*: Involves systems and technologies that enhance decision-making and strategic planning.

3. *Organizational Capital*: Pertains to the culture
    and processes that facilitate collaboration and
    adaptability.

These elements support the other perspectives by fostering a
sustainable environment for improvement. The financial perspective
measures profitability and cost management, while the customer
perspective focuses on satisfaction and retention. The internal processes
perspective evaluates operational efficiency and quality.

A core principle of the Balanced Scorecard is the equal emphasis
on financial performance and its underlying drivers, highlighting the
importance of continuous learning for maintaining competitive advantage.
This framework explicitly aligns performance metrics with organizational
strategy, ensuring that evaluations connect to broader objectives.

CHAPTER 4

Analyzing Business Performance with Google Analytics

KPIs and Performance Frameworks are continually in search of the right display tools. Google Analytics, which is by far the most popular, is the chosen display tool. Moreover, the latest version of Google Analytics, that is, GA4, with its embedded Google Cloud Platform (GCP), BigQuery database, and integrated Machine Learning Modeling capabilities, is in a position to predict what will happen, on top of reporting what has happened in the past.

The quest for a display tool is, in essence, the quest for incisive insights. Insights come in different flavors:

1. Visitor Acquisition Insights

2. Visitor Insights

3. Conversion Insights

4. User Experience Insights

© Suvradeep Bhattacharjee 2025
S. Bhattacharjee, *Path to Stellar Business Performance Analysis*,
https://doi.org/10.1007/979-8-8688-1501-0_4

Types of Insights and Examples from GA4

Visitor Acquisition Insights offer a strong framework for providing comprehensive support to effectively target, manage, and optimize your visitor acquisition strategy. This process begins with a thorough analysis of your current performance metrics, enabling a clear understanding of how your website currently attracts visitors.

The logical next step is to pinpoint crucial areas for enhancement which will attract most qualified visitors—those who are genuinely interested in your offerings rather than just casually browsing. You can increase your site traffic manifold by harnessing the incisive insights from your web analytics tools. More importantly, this traffic growth will be achieved by optimizing visitor acquisition costs.

The overarching rationale is not just to boost the number of visitors but also to encourage deeper and longer engagement with your target audience. The main goal is to equip you with the essential tools and knowledge. The end game is that you will build a strong online community that strengthens brand loyalty and develops lasting relationships with your customers.

Visitor Insights come from a comprehensive analysis of visitor behavior on your website, spotting essential patterns and trends that will give you first, the knowledge, and, then, the wisdom. By forensically examining this data, you can accurately trace the specific pathways that visitors take when navigating your site. Analysis of visitor paths helps you to identify which pages are most popular and the journey users undertake from entry to exit. To finish with "Cherry on the top," you can determine peak access times, which is crucial for understanding when your audience is most active.

Valuable information such as user engagement levels and user touch points can only be unveiled by tracking visitor actions during their time on your site using sophisticated web analytics tools such as Google Analytics 4. Google Analytics 4 helps you to analyze which content captures user interest, how long users stay on certain pages (i.e., Time on Page), and when they decide to leave. This understanding is absolutely pivotal to building an empathetic framework to align visitor interactions with your overarching business objectives. In other words, this understanding is like "Oxygen" for your website on an existential level.

This understanding of visitors' expectations is critical to enable a firm grip on a visitor's entire journey. To effectively meet visitor expectations, you must take decisive action to tailor your website design. This website redesign will involve improving content, enhancing navigation, and embedding interactive elements. In essence, leveraging these visitor insights will enable you to create a well-designed website that attracts visitors, engages them with stellar content plus smooth navigation, and converts them into happy customers.

Conversion Insights: Conversion from a visitor to a user is what makes your website, and, more importantly, your business, tick. Therefore, understanding the journey of your visitors is essential for your business's success. Identifying specific points where visitors disengage from the key processes you want them to complete is key. These processes could be navigating an online checkout counter, or filling out inquiries or contact forms, leading to new business opportunities.

These conversion insights are extremely valuable. These conversion details represent the overall objectives of your website. A detailed analysis of when, where, and how users abandon the crucial steps provides you with invaluable insights into their behavior and preferences. Understanding these insights can help you grasp the pain points during the visitor journey, as these pain points pose obstacles to the conversion of the visitor to a user.

Understanding the pain points will lead to crucial adjustments, such as simplifying the navigation process, improving the clarity of forms, or ensuring that the checkout experience is as seamless as possible. This can help you seize the opportunity to make strategic adjustments that enhance your user experience. Each enhancement in user experience will contribute massively to driving results that align with your overarching business goals such as increasing revenue.

User Experience Insights: Identifying pain points within user journeys is of strategic importance as this is crucial for assessing overall user experience. Can users quickly locate the information or products they seek without frustration? Alternatively, do they find themselves leaving your site searching for other options?

Analysis of visitor feedback is of vital importance. Visitor feedback comes in various forms. For example, direct responses through surveys, or indirect signals like article ratings, or, social media shares, or comments about your products or services. All this data can inform how users perceive their experience on your site.

The cost of a poor user experience is extremely high. No one enjoys the frustration of waiting for slow service, clicking on a link only to find it doesn't deliver as promised or landing on a page devoid of the content they were hoping to find. Such negative digital experiences are similar to poor in-person or phone interactions, leaving customers dissatisfied. Although, assessing the financial impact of a subpar digital experience is often more straightforward for organizations. Subpar user experience often leads to reduction in sales, reduced customer loyalty, and a damaged brand reputation.

Table 4-1 below captures my analysis of different types of insights:

Table 4-1. *Analysis of insights from GA4*

Type of insights	Situation	Problem	Solution
Visitor acquisition insights	Much awaited website redesign has little impact in attracting visitors to a clothing e-tailer's website	The loss of traffic occurred because the new website used different URLs in its architecture, while the search engine results still contained the old historical URLs.	By setting up custom alerts for error pages, the company could have detected the drop in organic traffic and revenue automatically within a few days— saving millions in lost revenue.
Conversion insights	A leading UK university is trying to understand the value of its website so that marketing budget can be properly planned.	How to assign a monetary value to a non-ecommerce website for a university?	Establish website engagement goals such as completion of request for information form. Assign a monetary value to each of the established website engagement goals.

(*continued*)

Table 4-1. (*continued*)

Type of insights	Situation	Problem	Solution
Conversion insights	A UK e-tailer is experiencing very little Return on Investment (ROI) from Google Ads	How do you correctly attribute sales to a particular set of user/visitor actions?	Last Click Attribution algorithm was distorting the real picture of how effective Google Ads was in converting visitors to customer through a purchase. Last Click Attribution algorithm should be replaced by a tailor-made attribution algorithm where more credit is given to the one who generated the lead as the initial lead is most valuable in a competitive and cut-throat retail market. Also, by the time of the last click, the purchasing decision has already been made.

GA4 Implementation and the Quest for Business Value

The most effective strategy for successfully completing GA4 implementation projects is to adopt a use-case-based approach. A well-defined use case provides a clear target that aligns the efforts of all stakeholders. Also, the use-case answers the crucial question of why the project is being undertaken.

On the contrary, adopting a solution without a sharp and clear use case is a recipe for disaster. Solutions based on a technology stack offer some promise of potential benefits but often lead to eventual disillusionment. Maintaining the focus and momentum is really hard when unforeseen operational costs begin to emerge and key internal advocates who championed the technology stack depart. Grounding the GA4 implementation project in a specific use case would give the implementation team a laser-sharp focus and would help to maintain the momentum.

Performance Analytics projects would hugely benefit from early and quick wins. As stakeholders see tangible results early on, their belief in the adopted methodologies is reinforced. This belief is critical because any depletion of trust in these processes early on can derail the entire performance analytics initiative. Ensuring early successes validates the adopted approach and fosters a positive environment for continued exploration and development in performance analytics.

Moreover, once you've completed the foundation, defer any non-essential features to the project's second phase. This would prevent scope creep. Document the project's technical requirements and organize them in a checklist format. Ensure that each requirement can be systematically verified and confirmed as completed at the end of the project. This approach will give focus and clarity throughout the development process.

Finding and Demonstrating Business Value

The best guarantee for the Performance Analytics project budget can be earned by finding and demonstrating the business value the project will bring. Therefore, it is critical to determine the revenue increase or cost savings your project is expected to generate. You can show this business value in a variety of ways:

- Assess how many hours employees spend on various tasks. Analyze this data to determine the average cost savings per hour when the task automation is fully operational. This is how you can illustrate the business value that automation will bring.

- Do not choose business metrics like "page speed" that are far removed from revenue generation or cost reduction. Instead, choose "total number of conversions," which easily translates to a potential increase in revenue if you multiply it by the average value of each conversion goal.

Assign a cash value to the use case at hand and assess the potential benefits your Performance Analytics project will bring. If the cost outweighs the potential benefits, abandon the current project and explore use cases where returns are promising.

Assessing Digital Maturity of the Firm Is Crucial

Assess the digital maturity roadmap spanning the next 1–3–5 years of your client organization. This would help guide your client toward better performance analytics capabilities and smarter business practices. More importantly, it will help you pitch your Performance Analytics projects better.

For example, don't pitch projects encompassing real-time machine learning capabilities to organizations that are reliant on traditional performance measures like bounce rate. Climbing to the summit requires gear, time, and most importantly, resolve.

Four Phases of a Performance Analytics Implementation Project

All Performance Analytics implementation projects include four elements that help you break down the phases of work:

Data Ingestion

This initial stage involves identifying the methods and processes by which data will enter the system. Typically, the data arrives in its raw form, requiring careful planning to ensure it can be accurately captured and subsequently transformed for analysis.

Data Storage

Storing the ingested data is the remit of the second phase. Easy retrieval and integration are of paramount importance. Data storage should be optimized considering the ease of data retrieval and the ease of data integration. Data organization should enable effective access through joins, transformations, and aggregations; making the ground ready for deeper analysis by data modelers.

Data Modeling

This is where the magic happens. This data modeling phase transforms the ingested data into a structured format where the underlying relationships, patterns, and insights from the ingested data are discovered. This resulting data model is the foundation for further analysis and is used in decision-making.

Data Visualization

In the final phase, the relevant and valuable insights derived from the data are mobilized into systems that can exert a tangible impact on the business. This means implementing strategies to ensure that the useful data is not only available but actively utilized to drive informed decision-making, enhance operational efficiencies, and optimize customer experiences.

GA4 mainly serve as a data source solution where it allows users to collect website and app data. Beyond the data collection capabilities, GA4's data import functionalities, such as the custom data imports and the Measurement Protocol, enable GA4 as the preferred choice for a data storage solution.

Moreover, GA4 demonstrate its data modeling capabilities through the availability of predictive metrics such as purchase probability, churn probability, and revenue prediction. These predictive insights will give you a better understanding of user behavior. Once these predictive metrics are harnessed, they can be exported to Audience segments under Google Ads where they can be used to deliver effective data visualizations.

It is important to note that the data modeling phase will not dominate the workload during a Performance Analytics project. In fact, the time consumed by the data modeling phase is often the smallest percentage of the overall project timeline. Instead, the time consumed by the data preparation (data ingestion + data storage) tends to dominate it significantly.

Distribution of Performance Analytics project time :

- *Data Ingestion*: 25% for gathering and importing data from various sources

- *Data Storage*: 35% for establishing secure databases and systems

- *Data Modeling*: About 15% for creating the framework and connections of the data

- *Data Visualization*: Approximately 25% for transforming data into report-ready formats

Understanding this distribution helps in managing expectations and prioritizing tasks during the performance analytics project life cycle.

To enhance efficiency, take advantage of the strengths each tool offers in your data workflow. While some data visualization tools have features for data import and transformation, they often struggle with complex data flows, leading to delays and frustration.

Instead, utilize BigQuery for data storage and transformation, as it excels in managing large datasets and executing complex manipulations. Once your data is optimized, export it to Data Studio for visualization. Although Data Studio can manage basic transformations, it isn't built for intricate joins or aggregations. By thoughtfully leveraging each tool's capabilities, you will enhance your data workflow and propel your performance analytics operations toward success.

Data Ingestion

The first stage in your data's journey begins with collecting the data from the many available sources. During data ingestion, you gather raw data from its origins, which include website interactions, social media activities, or email clicks. The methods selected for data ingestion are typically influenced by ownership and control.

First-party data refers to the information that you own and possess privately. This type of data is generated from your web analytics and internal sales or marketing systems. Your organization's digital maturity determines how well you can harness your own first-party data. Data quality issues often arise that can hinder the usability of your website.

Therefore, cleaning this data is one of the first tasks in order to make it actionable. For example, Google Analytics 4 (GA4) data fits nicely into this category.

For GA4, user interactions on your websites/apps/Internet-connected devices are called events, and this event data can go directly to GA4 through methods like custom events, recommended events, or the Measurement Protocol.

But there is one word of caution. Personally Identifiable Information (PII) such as name, address, email address, or telephone number should never be sent to GA4. If you need to use PII, the relevant data should come from your own proprietary systems.

second-party data is essentially some other company's first-party data which they are willing to share or sell. For example, data from Google Search Console shows how your customers are searching for your company online. You need to establish a formal agreement with companies like Google to access this second-party data, which is usually delivered through an API or in the form of a data export. You can enhance your first-party data by using this type of second-party data without sharing your own data with third parties. You can typically retrieve this second-party data using API calls, or through FTP exports, which require consideration of how your code is hosted to fetch the data effectively. In specific scenarios, such as utilizing the BigQuery Transfer service, the process may be streamlined to filling out a simple form provided the appropriate user permissions are in place. You often have the option to employ Software as a Service (SaaS) solutions for data linking, such as Supermetrics, Fivetran, or StitchData. Alternatively, you can construct your own API calls and execute them on a scheduled basis—commonly employing a blend of tools like Cloud Scheduler, Cloud Functions, Cloud Run, or Cloud Composer.

Third-party data is data received from a data aggregator. Common examples include weather data or industry benchmarks, which give context to your own data. This type of data can be gathered when collecting other data. For example, calling a weather API while collecting footfall data in a retail store to determine if the good weather has brought many shoppers to the store. This third-party data can also be acquired through scheduled API imports, similar to the method described above for second-party data. This third-party data will give you additional context dimensions for your existing performance analysis.

Also, please note that Personally Identifiable Information (PII) can accidentally end up in Google Analytics 4 (GA4) through URLs with email addresses from form submissions or user inputs in search boxes. Since GA4 has closed accounts for collecting PII, it's essential to carefully review your data practices to protect both your account and user privacy.

Finally, once you have identified potential data sources and learned how to import them effectively, the next step is to consider your data storage solutions. Please explore reliable and secure options that align with your data management needs.

Data Storage

When it comes to managing your data application, it's important to consider the origin of your data. You'll face a decision: whether to retain the data in its original storage location or to migrate it to a different system that you can fully control. For many regular use cases, the preferred choice is often BigQuery. This data warehouse entity provides a range of technical advantages, making it suited for data applications.

BigQuery is versatile as it has the ability to process both real-time data streams and batched data uploads, which keeps your data accessible and up-to-date. BigQuery is also cost-effective for data storage, offering a low financial commitment for accommodating large data volumes.

The ability of BigQuery to perform analytical queries on vast datasets (containing terabytes of data) while delivering results in a time frame that is not only reasonable but often impressive. BigQuery also integrates well with GA4, GCP, and other systems, providing a streamlined workflow across your data infrastructure. This combination of features makes BigQuery a strong contender for your data storage and processing needs.

While BigQuery serves a broad spectrum of use cases, it may not be the ideal choice for every application. For instance, if you need to retrieve information rapidly—such as looking up a user ID and fetching specific attributes in less than a second—BigQuery may fall short in meeting that requirement. In this specific case, Firestore can come to the rescue if you can transfer the relevant data from BigQuery into Firestore. Quicker access and retrieval of data would be possible by adopting this hybrid approach of using BigQuery and Firestore. This solution will be more suitable for performance analytics applications that demand immediate responses.

When considering your data storage needs, it's essential to address seven key questions that can shape your approach:

1. *Data Structure*: As a starter, assess whether your data is structured or unstructured. Structured data, such as that stored in databases with clearly defined formats (e.g., CSV or JSON), is easier to query. On the other hand, unstructured data includes formats that are not easily queried, for instance, images, videos, binary files, sound waves, or even unstructured CSV/JSON without a defined schema. A growing trend is leveraging machine learning to enhance the usability of unstructured data. By tagging images, for instance, you can effectively transform them into structured formats that are easier to analyze.

2. *Analytics Requirements*: Consider whether your data will undergo analytics. Analytics tasks generally focus on performing calculations swiftly, while operational data needs, such as serving website

content, prioritize quick access to individual records. To visualize this, think about how databases organize data: columnar storage excels at processing aggregate functions like SUMs and COUNTs rapidly, while row-based storage is more efficient for fetching specific individual records quickly.

3. *Transactional Data Updates*: Assess whether you will need to implement frequent updates typical of transactional systems. For example, financial applications might require real-time updates to user bank balances multiple times each hour, whereas operations like updating loan decisions might only need batch updates once a week. In such cases, ensuring ACID (Atomicity, Consistency, Isolation, Durability) compliance may be crucial to maintain the integrity of these transactions.

4. *Latency Expectations*: Do you require almost instantaneous results? If your applications demand responses in less than a second, then a traditional analytics database may not meet your needs efficiently.

5. *Integration with Mobile SDKs*: Will your data storage need to support mobile application integration? Platforms like Google Firebase offer specialized services designed for mobile data handling, allowing seamless connectivity with other mobile-friendly tools and services.

6. *Data Volume*: It's also important to gauge the volume of data you'll be processing. Knowing whether your data falls within the megabyte (MB),

terabyte (TB), or petabyte (PB) range will play a
critical role in determining the suitable data storage
solutions for your needs.

7. *Integration Capabilities*: Finally, look into how well
   your chosen data storage integrates with your data
   ingestion, modeling, and visualization workflows. A
   storage solution may meet many requirements, but
   if it's poorly positioned or has compatibility issues
   with your existing systems (leading to high costs for
   data importing/exporting), it may not be the best fit.
   This challenge often arises when you're attempting
   to consolidate data from multiple cloud locations
   for a single application. While most cloud providers
   can support application development, keep in mind
   the potential expenses involved in transferring data
   between different clouds.

By considering these factors, you can better tailor your data storage
strategy to meet your organization's requirements.

BigQuery offers a suitable solution for many use cases within Google
Cloud Platform (GCP) and Google Analytics 4 (GA4). The following seven
questions address some classic analytics workflows:

1. Is your data structured or unstructured?

   Most of the analytics data we handle is structured.
   This means that the data we handle conforms to a
   predefined schema. That makes it easier to analyze
   and manipulate the data.

2. Will you need to run analytics over your data?

   Absolutely. To derive insights and make informed
   business decisions, running analytics is essential.

3. Will you need transactional inserts?

    No, transactional inserts are not necessary in most
    analytics workflows. Most focus is on batch processing
    rather than real-time transaction handling.

4. Do you need low latency in results?

    Not for analytics workflows. In most cases, we
    prioritize comprehensive analysis over immediate
    results, allowing for more efficient data processing.

5. Will you be integrating your data with mobile SDKs?

    No, integrating with mobile SDKs is not a
    requirement for most projects.

6. How much data will you be using?

    We deal with data across all ranges. BigQuery
    efficiently handles both small and vast datasets.

7. How well will BigQuery integrate with your data
    ingestion/modeling/visualization needs?

    GA4 has a seamless and native integration with BigQuery,
    which simplifies workflows and enhances data collaboration.

    The responses to these questions highlight why BigQuery
    emerges as a strong choice for most performance
    analytics projects. Once you have established data flow
    into your chosen data storage solution, the next logical
    step is to focus on the structure of that data. This is where
    the real value comes. Creating a data model tailored
    to your use cases will enable actionable insights and
    informed decision-making. Approach this step with
    clarity to ensure your data serves its purpose effectively.

Data Modeling

The data modeling phase transforms the raw data acquired during the data ingestion phase into an organized format. This new data format aligns with specific use cases. This transformation performs four key functions. It filters out irrelevant information, aggregates data for better insights, performs statistical analyses to uncover trends, and applies machine learning techniques to derive predictive insights. This is where the magic happens.

Creativity and technical expertise come together, making it a crucial and highly personalized aspect of many performance analytics projects in this data modeling phase. It's often where the most innovative solutions emerge. This phase engages your specialized resources, particularly the skills and time of data scientists. This expertise is essential for this transformation process to succeed.

The data modeling involves a range of tasks, some simple, and some, extremely complex. Straightforward tasks include creating a clear and organized aggregate table. One leading example of intricate tasks is developing a real-time deep-learning neural network. Transforming raw data into valuable insights is the overarching mantra, regardless of the complexity of the tasks. More often than not, this process culminates in the generation of a well-structured flat table designed to facilitate the effective utilization of data through various activation channels.

Determining the level of accuracy for your data model is key. At first sight, it may seem that striving for the highest possible performance is the key. However, a deeper examination reveals that this assumption may not hold true in every scenario.

Establishing what constitutes a "good enough" metric for your model's performance is a good starting point. While it's natural for your data science team to pursue the highest accuracy rates, it's important to consider the concept of diminishing returns. A performance boost from

80% to 95% accuracy could demand significantly more effort, resources, and time, potentially doubling the investment. Conversely, aiming for a stellar 99% accuracy might require tenfold that effort, leading to considerable delays in project timelines.

Does your particular use case need a high level of precision? Is the additional accuracy worth extending the project timeline by an entire year? By answering these questions, you can align model performance with tangible business value.

Articulating the performance metrics required for the success of your use case is of paramount importance. Would achieving a higher level of accuracy translate into increased profitability for your business? Once you quantify this relationship between accuracy level and profitability, it will provide valuable insights into how you should allocate resources and time for your data science team. This clarity will help them focus on developing models that align with your specific goals, ensuring that their work is efficient and impactful.

The development of a functional model that can serve as an initial benchmark is highly beneficial. This allows you to establish a baseline for performance that can be evaluated over time. A precise and sophisticated model can be built with necessary resources and efforts after this model is successfully launched and operational. This iterative approach ensures that you gather valuable insights and feedback during the initial phase, which can inform future enhancements and improvements.

The complexity of the data modeling phase in the project largely hinges on the volume of data that needs to be transported to various destinations. Given the nature of web analytics data collection, it is probable that you will primarily be working with structured data during this modeling phase, likely housed within an SQL database. Using SQL to develop machine learning models is a challenging task as it requires a comprehensive understanding of the database system and intricate knowledge of the models themselves. Instead, the data scientists prefer to use Python, R, and Julia—more specialized programming languages which are designed for data analysis. These programming languages provide more robust tools and libraries to facilitate the data modeling work.

The advantages of moving data should be carefully assessed. A simple rule of thumb is to restrict data movement as little as possible. Transfer only the essential data required to fulfill your objectives. By following this rule, you can effectively reduce the risk of incurring high costs and mitigate issues related to data privacy. Also, this approach encourages thorough data cleaning at the source, ensuring that your data scientists have the bandwidth to focus on data analysis.

A well-defined brief for your data modelers is vital. The brief gives them a clear outline of the input data schemas they will work with. This brief should also specify the expected output data format to be produced by the end of the modeling process. The data modelers may engage in tasks such as performing joins between datasets, aggregating information, calculating statistics, and applying machine learning techniques, including neural networks. However, the core framework of the modeling endeavor will center around the input dataset they receive and the output dataset they are required to generate. By ensuring clarity in the brief, you help streamline the entire modeling workflow, making it easier to understand what is required and expected from the data modeling efforts.

Identifying the data visualization channel is crucial. It enables you to define the format in which the data will be displayed at the end. The data visualization channel needs to conform to certain specifications. For example, the data is to be ingested through an API (Application Programming Interface) for seamless integration or formatted as a CSV (Comma-Separated Values) file for straightforward import.

Creating a clean and organized working environment is vital. A more efficient workflow with datasets often results from an organized working environment. When everything is orderly, you can explore and analyze your data freely, without the constant interruptions of waiting for lengthy job processes to complete or seeking necessary authorizations. This streamlined approach enhances productivity and fosters a more innovative and collaborative atmosphere where bright ideas can flourish.

The following key elements should be included in the brief you are preparing for your data scientist to ensure clarity and alignment on the project objectives:

1. *Data Input Specification*: The expected format of the data input must be clearly outlined. A comprehensive data catalogue that defines each data point, providing insights into what they represent and how they will be used in the modeling process, is also necessary.

2. *Output Metrics*: You must specify the metrics and dimensions you expect to see in the modeled data. This includes key performance indicators (KPIs) or other statistical measures to help evaluate the data model's effectiveness.

3. *Success Metrics Threshold*: You should provide a threshold for success metrics associated with the data modeling project. For example, indicate that achieving predictions with more than 80% accuracy is necessary before the model will provide tangible business value.

4. *Frequency of Updates*: You should specify how frequently new model predictions or updates will be required. This depends on whether the data changes often or the business context evolves, impacting decision-making processes.

5. *Timeline for Initial Models*: Set a deadline for the initial models to enter the quality assurance (QA) phase. This will help manage expectations and keep the project on track.

6. *Deployment Details*: You should explain where the trained model will be deployed and the anticipated benefits of its implementation. This includes integrating the model into existing systems or using it for decision-making support in particular business areas.

7. *Prediction Timing*: You should indicate whether the predictions are needed in real time or if the predictions would be processed in batches. This distinction will help in designing the model and understanding the infrastructure requirements.

Including these detailed specifications in your brief will ensure that your data scientist understands the project goals and requirements, allowing for more effective collaboration and successful outcomes.

Developing machine learning models for predicting conversion rates must be accompanied by selecting the proper performance metrics to measure success. It's well-known that when working with unbalanced datasets, such as those involved in conversion rate predictions, relying on wrong accuracy levels can lead to massive misconceptions. For example, where conversion rates typically hover between 1% and 10%, a model could achieve an accuracy of 90% to 99% simply by predicting that no one will convert. This is not just misleading; it's outrageous.

Therefore, data scientists must diligently choose metrics that truly reflect a model's performance. They also need to understand the context in which the model's predictions will be used. In the case of conversion predictions, using accuracy alone is insufficient and can misrepresent a model's effectiveness. Instead, recall should be promoted as a key performance measure. Recall, which is defined as the ratio of correctly predicted conversions to the total number of actual conversions, provides a more accurate assessment of the data model's capability to identify positive outcomes. The choice of performance metrics is pivotal to ensuring that the data model delivers actionable insights that align with business goals and deliver business value.

Your data model's performance will decline over time after the model is deployed into a production environment. This decline occurs as the underlying data and the data model's context evolve. Establishing clear thresholds for your data model's key performance indicators (KPIs) is essential for managing this decline. These thresholds will serve as benchmarks to help you determine when to retrain the model using updated data. Retrain the model and if retraining does not yield satisfactory results, it may be necessary to rethink the modeling approach and explore alternative strategies. This proactive monitoring and adjustment process is essential to maintain the relevance and accuracy of your data model in a data and business landscape in flux.

The next logical step is determining how your data visualization will interact with your predictive data model to make predictions. This involves selecting innovative tools (such as Firestore, Cloud Build, and Cloud Composer) explicitly designed to facilitate the deployment and use of your predictive models in real-world applications. These tools can streamline the process of bringing your predictive data models into production, ensuring they are accessible and effective in generating insights from your data.

The primary challenge lies in ensuring that your newly acquired data can seamlessly integrate with your predictive model, enabling it to generate accurate predictions or insights. Even though the datasets used for training machine learning models can be quite extensive, the actual inputs needed to trigger predictions are often minimal—typically limited to a few key pieces of information like a user ID or a specific page visited.

When it comes to utilizing your models effectively, there are several established approaches:

1. *Create Your Model Where Your Data Resides*: Modern databases have evolved to become increasingly sophisticated, and allowed the creation of machine learning models directly within their environment. This eliminates the need for transferring data between training and production phases, streamlining the entire process. A prime example of this is BigQuery ML, which facilitates in-database model development.

2. *Upload Your Model to Where Your Data Lives*: In some cases, you might generate your machine learning model as an executable file or binary. You can then upload this model directly to the database where your data is stored, provided that the database supports such functionality. TensorFlow import feature from BigQuery ML exemplifies this method, enabling a smooth integration of the model with the data.

3. *Bring Your Data to Your Model*: You host your model on a platform and then send your data to that platform. This approach calls for a centralized

model management strategy. For example, users upload their data for analysis and predictions in Google's AutoML services.

4. *Develop an API to Access Your Model*: Create an API to retrieve results from your model by providing appropriate input data. This method is particularly versatile, allowing communication with any system that can make HTTP requests. A good example of this is the speech-to-text API, which highlights how machine learning models can be accessed and utilized across different applications.

These four approaches will help you increase the effectiveness of your predictive models in drawing meaningful insights from your data.

Data Visualization

When it comes to data projects such as GA4 implementation, one critical aspect that deserves significant attention is data visualization. This process is so crucial that it should be addressed right at the outset as part of the project's initial scope. While other phases of the project may be refined or developed later, data visualization must be considered from the beginning to ensure its effectiveness.

In this section, we will delve into various data visualization strategies, particularly in the realm of digital marketing, as Google Analytics 4 (GA4) continuously serves as a valuable source of insights ready for implementation.

Often, during performance analytics projects, data visualization is relegated to an afterthought, boiling down to the creation of a dashboard. But, dashboards are abandoned left, right, and center, where you discover that no one is engaging with the dashboards you have created with a lot of care, just after six months. I strongly advise against assuming a dashboard is the ultimate solution for showcasing your hard work. It's essential to explore and identify the most effective means of displaying the data, which will genuinely resonate with your audience and drive meaningful change.

One of my primary concerns with dashboards is the tendency of their creators to assume that their role ends once the dashboard is completed. There seems to be an expectation that viewers will automatically act on the data presented to them, as if the mere display of metrics and trends will spark a moment of realization. But that is overly simplistic, and this misconception grossly overlooks the inherent complexities of human behavior and the complex mechanics of how decisions are made.

If the ultimate goal is to drive meaningful change that showcases the business value of the insights provided, these dashboards must be deeply integrated into the overarching business strategy. This means that alongside the dashboard, there should be a robust framework of training sessions and leadership workshops to foster understanding and encourage engagement with the business performance data.

The dashboard should continually evolve with the changing needs of the business. Continuous refinement and adaptation are crucial to ensure that it remains relevant in guiding decision-making. This ongoing process requires commitment and collaboration, reinforcing that the value of a dashboard lies not just in the data it displays, but in the conversations, training, and strategic alignment it inspires.

I firmly believe that dashboards play a pivotal role in the initial phases of data visualization. However, the projects that have truly made a significant impact are those in which the insights derived from data modeling have actively influenced the strategies and behaviors of digital marketing channels. By effectively translating performance data into actionable changes, these initiatives transform the way marketing efforts are executed and optimized.

You should also assess other components of your marketing stack to gain a sound understanding of your capabilities. Consider whether you use a marketing automation tool, a customer data platform (CDP), or a customer relationship management (CRM) system. These platforms can send emails and integrate with your performance data modeling efforts. Particularly in the context of Google Analytics 4 (GA4), the Audiences feature is a powerful data visualization channel. "Audiences" can be exported directly to your paid media channels, enhancing your advertising strategies. By linking your data modeling process closely with these marketing activities, you significantly increase the potential to showcase persuasive use cases that yield results.

As we delve into digital marketing, it's crucial to recognize that our primary opportunities for impact reside within various digital marketing channels. Below are the six key channels you should focus on, along with suggestions on how to leverage data effectively to enhance our strategies:

1. *Organic Search and SEO*: To improve organic search visibility, we recommend conducting comprehensive keyword research to identify the terms potential customers are using. This can guide the creation of high-quality, relevant content tailored to match user queries. Additionally, generating landing page content that speaks directly to these keywords can enhance your click-through rates, driving more traffic to your site.

2. *Paid Search*: To ensure that your ads perform effectively, it's vital to continually optimize your keyword strategies and improve your quality scores. You can adjust your campaigns accordingly by staying responsive to current trends and shifting consumer behavior. Audience segmentation is critically essential, allowing you to target specific demographics more effectively and improve conversion rates.

3. *Email Marketing*: Leveraging audience segmentation is critical in personalizing your email marketing outreach. Understanding your audience's interests and behaviors allows you to create tailored content that resonates with them. Conducting thorough content research is another avenue to ensure that the information you share is engaging and relevant.

4. *Owned Media (Website)*: Focusing on your owned media, such as your website, requires a commitment to conversion rate optimization. This includes enhancing the user experience through faster page load times and personalized content that guides visitors through their journey. Effective design and usability can significantly impact how visitors interact with your site, leading to more conversions.

5. *Social Media*: Engaging actively on social media demands an eye for emerging trends that can capture the audience's attention. Personalized content that reflects the interests and preferences of your followers can foster deeper connections. Conducting robust content research allows you to create posts that engage and inform your audience, enhancing your overall brand presence.

6. *Display Advertising*: In display advertising, it's essential to regularly assess the quality of your ad placements and understand their effectiveness. A sense check should be in place to ensure that the right message is delivered to the right people. Refine

your segmentation strategies and target specific
audience segments more accurately to maximize the
impact of your advertising efforts.

By exploring and optimizing these digital marketing channels, you can
create a more cohesive strategy that aligns with your business goals and
enhances your overall marketing efforts.

In addition to enhancing your customers' experience, there is an
excellent opportunity to assist your colleagues and internal stakeholders in
performing their tasks with greater efficiency. Here are five sound ways to
achieve this:

Dashboards

Create visually appealing and informative dashboards that provide
decision support for employees. By aggregating and displaying relevant
data flows, these dashboards can empower staff with the insights they
need to make informed choices quickly.

Email Communication

Leverage personalized email communications to deliver valuable data
insights directly to employees. By tailoring the information to their specific
roles and needs, you can enhance their decision-making processes and
keep them informed of critical metrics and trends.

Automation

Implement automation to streamline repetitive tasks that consume
valuable time. By reducing the burden of mundane activities through
analyzing performance data, employees can redirect their energy toward
more strategic and impactful work, ultimately driving productivity and
innovation within the organization.

Human Resources (HR) Support

Utilize performance data analytics to monitor employee performance
and identify whenever they require assistance, particularly in cases where
you frequently encounter process bottlenecks. This proactive approach
allows HR to provide timely support and resources, helping smooth
workflow challenges and fostering a more switched-on workforce.

Stock Level Optimization

Adopt a data-driven approach to inventory management by accurately forecasting demand based on insights gathered from your marketing activities. This can help streamline the ordering process, ensuring that stock levels are optimized to meet customer needs while preventing overstocking and stockouts.

By embracing these approaches, you can foster a more efficient and collaborative work environment that benefits both employees and the organization as a whole. After activating your data modeling, you'll have the chance to revisit the initial business objectives and use case revenues. This process will allow you to assess how well your data model aligns with those objectives and to measure its overall impact on your use case revenue outcomes.

Summary

KPIs and Performance Frameworks are continually in search of the right display tools. Google Analytics, which is by far the most popular, is the chosen display tool. The quest for a display tool is, in essence, the quest for incisive insights. Insights come in different flavors:

1. Visitor Acquisition Insights

2. Visitor Insights

3. Conversion Insights

4. User Experience Insights

Performance Analytics implementation projects deliver these insights. All Performance Analytics implementation projects include four elements that help you break down the phases of work:

Data Ingestion

This first stage focuses on identifying how data will be gathered and entered into the system. Usually, data arrives in raw form, so it is important to plan carefully to ensure it can be accurately captured and later processed for analysis.

Data Storage

Storing the ingested data falls under the second phase. Prioritizing simple retrieval and seamless integration is essential. Data storage must be optimized to facilitate easy access and efficient data integration. Organizing data properly allows for effective joins, transformations, and aggregations, laying a strong foundation for advanced analysis by data modelers.

Data Modeling

This is where the magic happens. This data modeling phase transforms the ingested data into a structured format where the underlying relationships, patterns, and insights from the ingested data are discovered. This resulting data model is the foundation for further analysis and is used in decision-making.

Data Visualization

In the final phase, the key insights gained from the data are integrated into systems that can make a real business difference. This involves deploying strategies to ensure that valuable data is not just accessible but actively used to support informed decisions, improve operational efficiency, and enhance customer experience.

GA4 primarily functions as a data source, allowing users to collect data from websites and apps. In addition to data collection, GA4's data import features—such as custom data imports and the Measurement Protocol— make it an ideal option for data storage solutions.

Moreover, GA4 demonstrate its data modeling capabilities through the availability of predictive metrics such as purchase probability, churn probability, and revenue prediction. These predictive insights will give you a better understanding of user behavior. Once these predictive metrics are harnessed, they can be exported to Audience segments under Google Ads where they can be used to deliver effective data visualizations.

It is important to realize that the data modeling phase does not take up most of the workload in a Performance Analytics project. In fact, it usually accounts for the smallest portion of the total project timeline. More significantly, the bulk of the time is spent on data preparation activities such as data ingestion and data storage.

CHAPTER 5

Deep Dive into Google Analytics Data Visualization

Data visualization represents a crucial cornerstone of the Performance Analysis project, where we aim to achieve return on investment, make a significant impact, and create value. In this chapter, I will explore various applications of data visualization, primarily defined as the use of data to guide business decisions and influence user behavior. These mean real change.

A Performance Analysis project lacking the capacity for change holds no real power and may as well be non-existent. Influence can be exerted in various forms: it might manifest as a singular insight that the CEO considers during budget allocations, a daily metric tracking tool for performance analysts to determine their next focus, or an automatically updating website feature that modifies prices or content in real time. All of these examples qualify as data visualization, although the effectiveness and measurability may vary from one to another.

As a result, data visualization is essential if you want to take Performance Analysis projects beyond mere education or as a proof of concept. It's vital to outline your data visualization strategy during the project scoping, which we will discuss further in the next section.

© Suvradeep Bhattacharjee 2025
S. Bhattacharjee, *Path to Stellar Business Performance Analysis*,
https://doi.org/10.1007/979-8-8688-1501-0_5

Benefits of Data Visualization

While data visualization is often overshadowed by data modeling, I believe it is crucial—it's better to have a subpar model with strong visualization than a solid model with weak visualization. If you find yourself only considering data visualization after completing data modeling, or if you presume a dashboard will naturally follow without questioning that belief, it may indicate a lack of proper focus on visualization. In this section, I will present key concepts that will assist you in determining the most effective approach for your performance analysis projects.

When planning your performance analysis projects, it's essential to understand the potential benefits for your business. This typically involves estimating the value that the additional data visualization phase can bring, which often manifests as cost savings or increased revenue. Here are some techniques to help estimate these figures:

Efficiency leading to time savings

A shared objective is to automate an action that your colleagues handle, which can be optimized through an automated service. For instance, consolidating all metrics into a single location allows users to log in once to access the information they need, instead of spending hours each week logging into various services, downloading data, and manually aggregating it in a spreadsheet. This approach enables you to estimate cost savings by calculating the monthly hours saved and multiplying that by the average hourly rate of those users.

Enhancing the return on investment for marketing expenditures

With GA4 emphasizing digital marketing, a key objective is to enhance your conversion and click-through rates by offering a more relevant website or advertisement experience for customers. If your project can be credited for this increase, you can calculate a corresponding rise in revenue based on standard monthly traffic volumes.

Reducing marketing costs

A comparable visualization approach might aim to reach the same number of customers more effectively, reducing your spending to attract that same audience. A frequent method involves customizing the keywords you target through paid search or geotargeting those users while excluding customers you believe are unlikely to make a purchase (such as existing customers). This way, you could credit the decreased incremental costs each month to your performance analysis project.

Minimizing customer churn

Certain performance analysis initiatives are validated by their ability to enhance customer satisfaction, leading to a rise in repeat purchases and a decrease in churn. This can be achieved through personalization or by identifying and eliminating bothersome sales tactics affecting current customers. Research indicates that acquiring a new customer can be ten times more expensive than retaining an existing one, which allows you to connect this cost or the potential revenue increase from repeat customers back to your project.

Gaining new customers

Most businesses require a continuous influx of new customers. Therefore, identifying new customer segments beyond your current base can be extremely valuable, particularly for growing startups. Developing look-alike audiences to find potential customers similar to your existing ones, or conducting keyword research for users seeking comparable products, could provide motivation for your data project. Competitor analysis may also play a role here. Ultimately, you can correlate any increase in new customer signups to the insights gained from your performance analysis project.

Often, the value you can add through data visualization amounts to an informed estimate. Nevertheless, having a rough estimate is crucial for comparing your expectations with reality and securing approval for any necessary budget related to the project. This process will help you determine the required resources and essential data, and you'll discover that it serves as a key point of interaction between your organization's business and technical faculties.

One key reason that many companies choose Google Analytics is its seamless integration with Google Ads and the broader Google Marketing Platform (GMP). GA4 stands out due to this integration ability compared to other analytics platforms, particularly since Google Ads serves as a primary channel for digital marketing for many users.

The GMP encompasses these solutions and roles:

GA4
Measurement and analytics for websites and mobile applications.
Data Studio
This is a free online data visualization tool that integrates with various Google services, such as Google Analytics and BigQuery. It is frequently used to create a presentation layer that combines your GA4 data with other sources.
Optimize
An A/B testing and personalization tool for your website. This tool adjusts the content that visitors view and tracks their activity to determine if goals like improved conversion rates are achieved through statistical modeling.
Tag Manager
This is a JavaScript container that resides on your website, allowing you to manage all your other JavaScript tags from a single location without requiring website updates each time. It features helpful triggers and variables typically used for analytics tracking, including scroll and click tracking.
Campaign Manager 360
A centralized digital media management platform utilized by advertisers and agencies to dictate the timing and placement of digital ads.

Display & Video 360

Utilized by companies aiming to promote on video and display networks. Assists users in creating ads, acquiring them, and enhancing campaign performance.

Search Ads 360

Utilized by companies aiming to promote keywords across search engines such as Google Ads, Bing, and MSN.

All these platforms serve as data visualization channels, except for GA4 and Tag Manager, which function primarily as data ingestion tools. A major advantage of the GMP is that audiences can be generated in GA4 and subsequently exported (with consent) to other services. This indicates that information gathered with GA4, like user preferences, can impact the media they encounter on other platforms, including video and search.

GA4 audiences allow you to aggregate collected metrics, user properties, and dimensions into segments that share similar characteristics. Initially, they aid in analysis, helping to identify all individuals who have purchased or viewed specific content. You can include several criteria to define very specific audiences. Their effectiveness increases significantly when integrated with other services, as they can then be utilized to customize content or website behavior for that specific subset of users.

The integrations for data visualization in GA4 are likely the primary reason to choose GA4 over other analytics tools, particularly if your business utilizes other Google digital marketing services like Google Ads. This feature sets the product apart and is a major factor behind Google Analytics being free.

Google understands that the better you can measure the success of your digital marketing efforts, the more inclined you will be to allocate a larger budget to Google Ad services. Many of these data activation capabilities are available through Audiences, allowing you to segment users and export those attributes to platforms such as Google Optimize or Google Ads.

After you create your Audience in GA4, you can visualize it by exporting it to your selected GMP service. One option is Google Optimize, which I will explore next.

Google Optimize

Google Optimize is a website testing tool that enables you to deliver different content to various users to determine which version performs the best. It helps you evaluate your hypotheses regarding improvements for your website's performance. For instance, if you suspect that a red "Add to Cart" button may confuse customers unfamiliar with that color for this type of action, you might consider changing it to green to increase conversions. However, if your assumption is incorrect, you want to avoid accidentally decreasing your revenue. By using an A/B testing tool like Google Optimize, you can compare these two versions directly by showing one variation (A) to some users and the other variation (B) to others. Analyzing the performance data of both will help identify the optimal choice. Google Optimize allows you to temporarily modify your website's appearance for testing these variations while ensuring that each visitor consistently sees the same version. Its features also include targeting specific content to distinct audiences or segments, including those defined in your Google Analytics GA4 audiences.

After you connect your Google Optimize and GA4 accounts, you'll need to add a JavaScript snippet to manage the content Google Optimize displays on your site, followed by linking your GA4 account. Once everything is installed and linked, your GA4 Audiences will begin appearing in Google Optimize. When you've created your website content, you can choose who sees it by selecting your GA4 Audiences.

Making Dashboards Work

Dashboards are built on an essential assumption: that the viewer will analyze the data, gain insights, and subsequently use those insights to inform data-driven decisions within the company. This assumption is challenging to fulfill and should not be taken for granted. Achieving this outcome necessitates certain conditions:

The correct data is delivered to the dashboard.

This explains the technical workflow for loading data into the dashboard. Depending on the number of data sources being utilized, the process can range from straightforward to complex. While this is often mistakenly viewed as the sole significant task for data visualization, there are additional factors to consider.

The data is relevant when viewed.

A typical dashboard project begins by scoping with the intended user regarding the dashboard's purpose. Nonetheless, in many businesses, this purpose is dynamic; therefore, the initial scope may become outdated by the project's conclusion. This is often reflected in the significant drop in login frequency to dashboards over time. One potential solution is to increase the dashboard's interactivity or transform it into an analytical tool, incorporating elements of self-service that allow end users to keep the data relevant.

The data is presented clearly for easy user comprehension.

This field is intricate and multifaceted, incorporating elements of design, user experience, and data interpretation psychology. It frequently happens that two individuals can examine the same data and arrive at conflicting conclusions due to their unique contexts. Maintaining a focused and straightforward dashboard should be a primary goal; however, this can conflict with the need to make the dashboard applicable to various situations, leading users to display numerous data points simultaneously.

The user trusts the data.

End users can quickly lose confidence in the reliability of data, even if its technical quality is flawless. A few timeouts, processing errors, or inaccurate inputs can render the entire project ineffective. Sometimes, the issue stems from data providing answers that users find unsatisfactory. Addressing this requires extensive communication and creating highly resilient data pipelines.

The user possesses sufficient agency to act on that data.

A performance analyst might have an ideal dashboard, but if they are unable to persuade their boss or other stakeholders about the insights derived from it, it won't affect the business's bottom line. Selecting the appropriate stakeholders to develop your data products for is an essential part of the scoping process.

If you can confirm that you meet all these criteria, you're likely good to go ahead with creating your dashboard, but it's important to review it regularly to maintain its relevance. For your data visualization requirements, we will first explore the options available in GA4, followed by some advanced offerings, including Google Looker Studio.

GA4 Dashboarding Options

The GA4 web interface offers two distinct reporting models that can be confusing when compared. Think of these as two separate categories for data presentation, each with its own interpretation rules. Standard Reports can be found under the Reports tab and provide general aggregates for straightforward reporting, but they do not include segmentation or filtering options. On the other hand, Exploration Reports, accessible from the Explore tab, offer advanced analytical features like segmentation, filters, funnels, and pathing, though they may experience sampling issues.

GA4 Reports

The "Reports" section of GA4 offers a comprehensive summary, consolidating the daily trends from the event data you send, as shown in Figure 5-1. Unlike Exploration Reports, these reports serve a different purpose.

Figure 5-1. *GA4 Standard Reports*

The reports in the Reports section can be tailored through the Library section located at the bottom of the menu bar. As time progresses, new customizable reports will become available for end users upon logging in. This functionality will assist you in restricting Reports to those that are pertinent to the user logging in.

Figure 5-2. *GA4 Standard Reports Library*

Reports provide a helpful overview of your website's performance, but there are times when deeper exploration and data manipulation are necessary. If GA4 Reports don't yield the insights you need, try using the Exploration module, which I will discuss in the next section.

GA4 Explorations

To access GA4 Explorations, log into GA4 through the Explore menu located at the top left. These explorations are ideal for generating ad hoc data analysis reports and utilize features like sorting, drilldowns, filters, and segments. Additionally, you can use them to create GA4 Audiences for other GMP services. Here's a suggested workflow for using them:

1. *Create Exploration*: Create or select an existing report or template Exploration, such as the reports that come by default. This is the context for the use case you want to analyze. You can see the start screen in Figure 5-3.

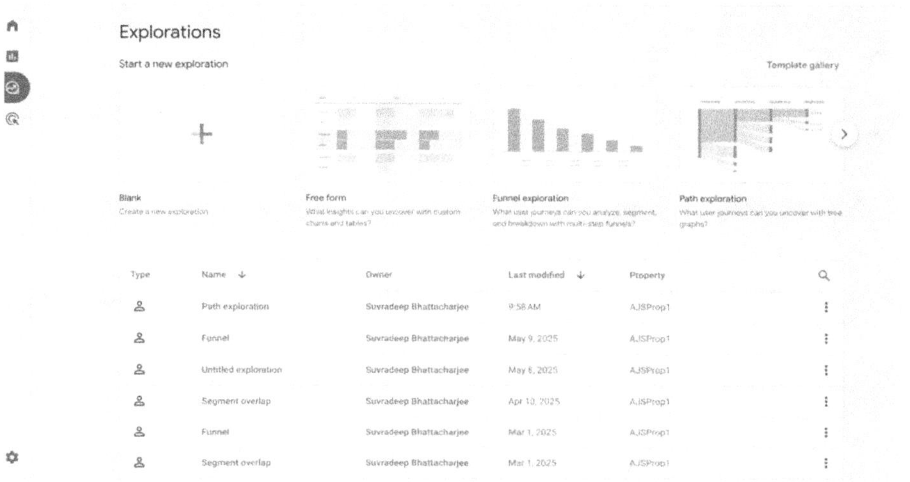

Figure 5-3. *The start of your Exploration workflow*

2. *Select Variables*: In the Variables section, click the
    + button to add or remove the specific segments,
    dimensions, and metrics you may need. This helps
    you concentrate on only the necessary items,
    preventing information overload, as illustrated
    in Figure 5-4. You can adjust these fields later if
    required.

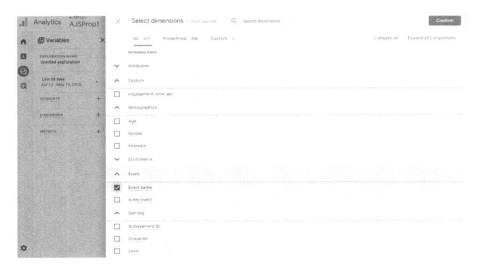

Figure 5-4. *Selecting the variables*

3. *Choose Technique*: Choose the analysis technique
    in the next tab column. These range from tables,
    funnel explorations, path graphs, and segment
    overlap plots. The techniques all have different
    functionalities. For instance, in Figure 5-5, right-
    clicking on segment overlaps allows you to further
    deep-dive into those users or create an Audience
    and subsegment from them.

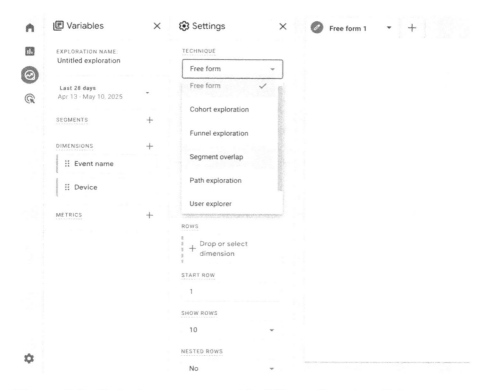

Figure 5-5. *Technique- reports with different functionalities*

4. *Review and Analyze*: Go through the previous steps
   again to include additional fields, segments, and
   filters that help you access the information you
   need. When you're prepared, you can choose to
   share the data with another GA4 user or export it to
   PDF or Google Sheets.

Your analysis heavily relies on a range of Exploration techniques,
which include an expanding selection of tools featuring right-click
interactivity to facilitate the "flow" of your analysis. Given that these
techniques play a crucial role in deriving insights from your GA4 data,

here's a concise overview of the available methods and their features you might find useful:

Free-form exploration

This is usually where you begin, as it offers a standard table along with plotting options like line, scatter, bar, and geo reports. Utilizing line charts will enable time-series features such as anomaly detection, which identifies when your measurements experienced unusual activity.

User exploration

This report allows you to examine individual users in great detail, as demonstrated in Figure 5-6. You can explore users within a specific segment to identify the events they triggered. Additionally, you have the option to delete user data if needed. A valuable use case is to segment users to pinpoint typical behaviors you aim to target, such as those who did not complete a purchase after clicking a specific internal banner. You can then identify similar users and create an Audience to target them, potentially through an A/B test using "Google Optimize."

Figure 5-6. *User Exploration*

Segment Builder

This technique enables you to visualize Venn diagrams of your segments and assists you in creating subsegments. Figure 5-7 illustrates an example.

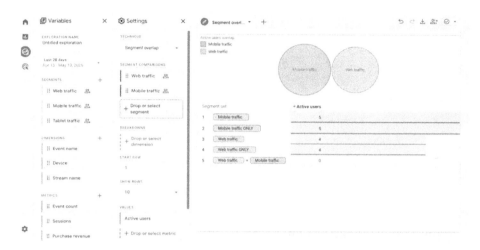

Figure 5-7. *Segment Builder*

Path exploration

This enables you to address user flow inquiries like, "Where did users go after visiting this page?" Since GA4 operates on an event-driven model, it extends to questions such as, "What events occurred following this click/ view/purchase?" The term "after" can refer to actions within the same session or over multiple sessions, allowing you to combine event names with page titles.

Figure 5-8. *Path analysis*

Funnel exploration

Funnels are widely used in digital marketing to depict the user journey across different pages, such as from a product page to the basket and then to the payment page until completion. It's believed that users start at the top of the funnel (the initial page) and navigate through predictable stages to reach the end. A typical optimization strategy is to enhance this journey, aiming to reduce the number of users who abandon the process (or skip to the next step), which helps in boosting conversion rates. This approach is connected to path analysis but pays more attention to user drop-off rates as they move through the defined funnel stages. This is often where optimization opportunities lie, such as enhancing click-through or ecommerce conversion rates, providing a foundational area for determining future data project priorities. Funnel steps can consist of both events and page views. Additionally, users can right-click within the funnel visualization to access a User Exploration report detailing who exited, as illustrated in Figure 5-9.

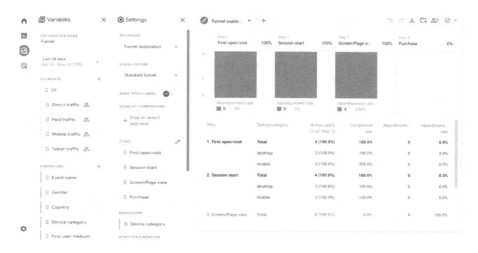

Figure 5-9. *Funnel exploration*

Cohort exploration

Cohorts focus more on categorizing users than on the frequency of their visits or returns to your website. This approach can aid in assessing your website's "stickiness" and may serve as a key performance indicator (KPI) for publisher websites dependent on ad revenue. You can analyze the cohorts by different segments and dimensions and determine the criteria for when a user is initially recognized as a visitor.

Figure 5-10. *Cohort Exploration*

This section examined the different visualization options available in the GA4 interface. However, you may decide against using GA4's reports if you already have your own visualization tools and workflows, prefer not to provide access to GA4, or want to retain business users in a more controlled environment.

Summary

Data visualization is crucial for advancing Performance Analysis projects beyond basic education or proof of concept. It's important to define your data visualization approach early in the project planning stage. When designing your performance analysis initiatives, understanding their potential value to your business is key. This usually means assessing how much the extra data visualization can contribute, often resulting in cost reductions or revenue growth. Here are some methods to help quantify these benefits:

1. Efficiency leading to time savings

2. Enhancing the return on investment for marketing expenditures

3. Reducing marketing costs

4. Minimizing customer churn

5. Gaining new customers

Google Analytics (GA4) is undoubtedly the data visualization tool of choice. The integrations for data visualization in GA4 are likely the primary reason to choose GA4 over other analytics tools, particularly if your business utilizes other Google digital marketing services like Google Ads. This feature sets the product apart and is a major factor behind Google Analytics being free. One key reason that many companies choose Google Analytics is its seamless integration with Google Ads and the broader Google Marketing Platform (GMP). GA4 stands out due to this integration ability compared to other analytics platforms, particularly since Google Ads serves as a primary channel for digital marketing for many users.

Data Visualization is often synonymous with Dashboarding. Dashboards are built on an essential assumption: that the viewer will analyze the data, gain insights, and subsequently use those insights to inform data-driven decisions within the company. This assumption is challenging to fulfill and should not be taken for granted. Achieving this outcome necessitates certain conditions:

1. The correct data is delivered to the dashboard.

2. The data is relevant when viewed.

3. The data is presented clearly for easy user comprehension.

4. The user trusts the data.

5. The user possesses sufficient agency to act on that data.

If you confirm that you meet all these criteria, you can probably proceed with creating your dashboard. However, it's important to review it regularly to keep it relevant.

CHAPTER 6

The Making of the User Experience

Life is about connection, and the User Experience (UX) is no different. Your work needs to nurture your own spirit and those of your users. Even when working on a product with no apparent connection, you will serve your users best if you keep that possibility present. I believe UX work speaks to the human spirit. That's why website and app design need UX. That's why insights delivered by GA4 need the help of UX professionals to bring about meaningful change, which will transform business performance by emotionally affecting the users.

Emotional Impact Is Part of the UX

The emotional aspects of user experience include the whole palette of emotions, which are the affective parts of user interaction: pleasure, fun, aesthetics, novelty, originality, sensations, and experiential features. In particular, it is about the emotional impact of the interaction on the user, which subliminally influences the user's behavior.

© Suvradeep Bhattacharjee 2025
S. Bhattacharjee, *Path to Stellar Business Performance Analysis*,
https://doi.org/10.1007/979-8-8688-1501-0_6

*Users are no longer satisfied with efficiency and effectiveness;
they are also looking for emotional satisfaction.*

—Shih and Liu (2007)

The Potential Coverage of Emotional Impact

Sometimes, a user's reaction to a system or product is extremely emotional, creating a user experience with a deep, intimate, and personal impact. At other times, a user might feel mildly satisfied (or dissatisfied) or just a bit pleased. Not all user experiences evoke throes of ecstasy, nor should they. Often, simply being well satisfied without rising to a personally emotional level is all a user can afford regarding emotional involvement with a website or app.

However, we all live for the moments when the user experience reaches its high note of emotional impact, when I experience amazingly cool products (websites rarely reach these heights). I am referring to a website or app that sets the user experience apart, making it stand out in the hearts and minds of discriminating users.

While other similar products may have an equally usable and useful design, they lack that something extra that sparks a deep emotional chord of affinity. The others do not possess that indefinable something that transcends form, function, usability, and usefulness—something that elevates the user experience to pure joy and pleasure, akin to the appreciation of well-crafted music or art.

Journey from Usability to User Experience

Human–computer interaction (HCI) refers to the collaboration between a human user and a computer system aimed at achieving a specific goal. Usability, a key component of HCI, focuses on making this interaction effective, efficient, and enjoyable for the user. It encompasses traits like ease of use, productivity, efficiency, effectiveness, learnability, retainability, and user satisfaction (ISO 9241-11, 1997).

While usability increasingly establishes itself in the tech sector, several misconceptions persist. Firstly, usability should not be confused with what some refer to as "dummy proofing." Although it may have seemed somewhat charming initially, this term is offensive to both users and designers. Additionally, usability is not synonymous with being "user-friendly." This misinterpretation oversimplifies the vast scope of the interaction design process and downplays the importance of user performance in terms of productivity, among other factors. As a user, I seek not just friendliness but a tool that is efficient, effective, safe, and perhaps even aesthetically pleasing and enjoyable, enabling us to achieve our objectives.

For those unfamiliar with the field, "doing usability" is often mistakenly equated with usability testing. Although usability evaluation is crucial—perhaps even central—in the process of interaction design, it indeed does not encompass everything involved in creating and refining interaction design, as I will explore in this chapter.

Interaction design has transformed, moving away from a strictly engineering perspective centered on user performance and usability to a more comprehensive view of user experience. Like many emerging concepts, it requires time for supporters to reach a consensus on its meaning (Dagstuhl, 2010).

As a field evolves, it's common to strive for broad aims. For instance, Thomas and McCredie (2002) advocate for a "new usability" that addresses "new design requirements such as ambience or attention." During a Special Interest Group (SIG) meeting at CHI 2007 (Huh et al., 2007), the conversation emphasized "exploring diverse approaches (beyond usability) like user experience, aesthetic interaction, ambiguity, slow technology, and different methods to comprehend social, cultural, and contextual factors in our environment."

117

Some argue that focusing on emotional factors is not a new idea—user satisfaction, a longstanding subjective measure of usability, has always been integral to the traditional usability concept recognized by many, including the ISO 9241-11 standard definition. Additionally, user satisfaction questionnaires assess users' emotions or opinions. As noted by Hazzenzahl et al. (2000), particularly in practice and as shown in many usability questionnaires, this form of user satisfaction is considered a consequence of users' experiences regarding usability and usefulness.

Consequently, the user satisfaction questionnaires have prompted responses that lean more toward the intellectual rather than the emotional; they have typically not addressed what I refer to as emotional impact. I have emphasized objective user performance metrics like efficiency and error counts, more than these aspects. Technology and design have progressed from mere productivity tools to elements that are more personal, social, and intimate in our lives. Thus, I require a much broader understanding of what defines quality in our designs and the quality of the user experiences resulting from those designs.

When all else is equal, a product that offers a superior user experience typically sells better than one with greater functionality. While many factors influence a product's market share, user experience stands out as the most critical among similarly capable options. Notable examples, such as the iPod, iPhone, and iPad, illustrate that the market transcends mere features; it prioritizes thoughtful design that enhances the user experience as the key to accessing functionality.

Many users think they receive accurate and comprehensive functionality from their software, but they perceive this capacity solely through the interface. For them, the interaction experience shapes the system. Furthermore, traditional usability is still crucial. Users have a limit to their efforts, beyond which they might abandon the task and fail to achieve the desired functionality. Larry Marine (1994) stated: "If the users can't use a feature, it effectively does not exist." He addresses usability testing for a new system version, pointing out user feedback expressing a desire for a feature in the current system and how frequently they would use it. However, the existing product already included this feature, prompting designers to question why users asked for something they already had. The reason was clear: users did not have access to it.

Hassenzahl and Roto (2007) discuss the difference between usability's functional view and the phenomenological view of emotional impact. People use technical products because "they have things to do" such as making calls, writing documents, shopping online, or searching for information. They refer to these as "do goals," assessed by usability and usefulness measures of "pragmatic quality." Additionally, users have emotional and psychological needs related to self-identity, social connections, and life satisfaction, termed "be goals," evaluated by emotional impact and phenomenological measures of "hedonic quality."

The phenomenological aspects, stemming from phenomenology, which philosophically examines the foundations of experience and action, represent the long-term, cumulative emotional impacts. In this context, web and mobile technology become significant in our lives, shaping the meaning we derive from our experiences.

Components of a User Experience

I would like to highlight that usability remains essential despite the growing prominence of user experience concepts. Important usability aspects, such as ease of use and learnability, are still critical for the majority of websites and applications. This is especially true in intricate work environments, where it is crucial for users to complete tasks efficiently, effectively, and with minimal errors or frustration. The evolving notion of user experience continues to integrate these usability elements. For example, how enjoyable is a well-designed iPad if it's challenging and cumbersome to use? Clearly, the satisfaction gained from using a website or mobile app is closely tied to its usability.

As a result, I have expanded the scope of user experience to include:

- Effects experienced due to **usability factors**
- Effects experienced due to **usefulness factors**
- Effects experienced due to **emotional impact factors**

The Making of the "Visitor Experience"

Various design qualities influence the user experience on a website, extending beyond usability. I prefer to refer to it as "visitor experience" when designing a web user interface. Additionally, I acknowledge that at least five distinct website qualities can affect visitors' experiences:

1. Utility
2. Functional integrity
3. Usability
4. Persuasiveness
5. Graphic design

UTILITY

Utility is often an overlooked aspect of website design that significantly influences visitor experience, as it is one of the most fundamental qualities. The utility of a website refers to how useful, necessary, or engaging its content, whether information, products, or services, is for visitors. This is inherently subjective; what you find interesting or beneficial might not hold the same value for someone else. Additionally, utility is dynamic; some websites will seem more useful or engaging than others depending on individual perception. For instance, some visitors enjoy social networking platforms like YouTube or Facebook, while others see them as a complete waste of time. I might not need a website that sells gardening tools, but my friend would likely use such a site regularly. This emphasizes a crucial point for designers: a single design can yield varied visitor experiences due to the differences among website users. Therefore, it is essential to design specifically for a target audience, informed by a strong understanding of that group.

FUNCTIONAL INTEGRITY

A website's *functional integrity* reflects how effectively it performs as intended. Issues such as "dead" links that lead to nowhere, freezing or crashing during specific actions, improper display across various browsers or their versions, and unintentional downloads of unwanted files can compromise functionality. A lack of functional integrity often points to faulty, erroneous, or even malicious coding. This aspect is not fixed; while some websites may only have minor bugs, others could be largely ineffective, with many variations in between. Additionally, the functional integrity of a site may differ for visitors using different browsers or browser versions.

USABILITY

Usability primarily concerns how easy it is for both first-time and occasional visitors to learn and for regular users to use a website. A site might offer high utility and impressive functional integrity, yet still present significant learning challenges or feel cumbersome to navigate. For example, the online portal used to file tax returns may be perfectly coded and relevant for nearly every adult, providing substantial convenience and cost savings; however, many users could find it exasperatingly hard to learn or inefficient to operate. Conversely, a website might appear very user-friendly but may not be particularly beneficial for a specific individual or could lack functional integrity. It may be simple and intuitive to understand how to execute a task, yet the site might often crash at a certain point in the task sequence, making it impossible to complete the task.

PERSUASIVENESS

Persuasiveness indicates how effectively a website's visitor experience fosters specific behaviors known as "conversions." The definition of a conversion differs across websites, and even non-eCommerce sites can support various types of conversions, such as signing up for a newsletter, switching to online tax filing, or accessing medical information. However, persuasiveness is especially vital in e-commerce design, where the primary conversion is a sale. Thus, for e-commerce websites, persuasiveness primarily focuses on how well the visitor's experience drives and promotes sales.

Two examples of persuasive elements center around the presence, quality, and placement of two types of information: *vendor* details (like company name, physical address, contact details, company history, and customer testimonials) and *product* information (such as product color, material, care instructions). Visitors desire reassurance that they can trust an online vendor, especially if they are unfamiliar with it. Additionally, many are reluctant to buy a product without sufficient information to determine whether it meets their needs. This is why many individuals first turn to `www.amazon.co.uk` , a well-regarded vendor known for providing comprehensive product details and thorough reviews from other customers. It's crucial to recognize that while a website may operate effectively and aid users in completing tasks, the absence of vital persuasive elements—such as sufficient vendor and product information—can lead to lost sales. This loss not only impacts the website owner but also frustrates visitors, impeding their objectives and detrimentally affecting their overall experience.

GRAPHIC DESIGN

Ultimately, a website's "look and feel"—particularly its *graphic design*—greatly affects the user's experience. The graphic design, which encompasses elements like colors, images, and other media, triggers emotional reactions in visitors, either aligning with or hindering the site's goals. Just as with other design elements that impact users, personal responses to graphic design can differ. While you may consider soft pastel colors boring, I might find them soothing and comforting. Likewise, a basic and clear graphic design could come across as lacking inspiration for you but may seem professional and reliable to me. What I find unappealing, such as sound and animation, may be thrilling and very attractive to you.

Interplay of Five Website Qualities

Although utility and functional integrity are primarily distinct design qualities, the differences between usability, persuasiveness, and graphic design are not as apparent. Both usability and high-quality graphic design can improve the feeling of persuasiveness, while graphic design significantly impacts usability as well. Nevertheless, analyzing these design qualities separately helps in understanding their importance and applying them effectively during the design process.

Crafting an outstanding visitor experience requires a specialized team. *Market research,* a traditional field, is key to ensuring *utility.* Competent w*eb develope*rs are necessary for upholding *functional integrity.* Proficiency in s*oftware and web usability engineering* is crucial to improving *usability.* A new wave of professionals is now employing marketing and *persuasion psychology* in e-commerce website design. Finally, *graphic design*ers specializing in website design bring vital expertise in branding and audience engagement that websites depend on.

Success hinges on building an effective interdisciplinary design team, rather than merely selecting individuals with the necessary skills. Professionals from different fields often lack a deep understanding of each other's disciplines, which can hinder their ability to collaborate effectively to create the best visitor experience for a specific target audience. At a minimum, stakeholders should ensure that members of the product development team appreciate one another's expertise and are willing to learn, promoting effective collaboration aimed at designing an optimized experience for intended website visitors. By harnessing their varied knowledge, experts from different backgrounds can greatly improve website success, providing a positive experience for the target audience.

User experience refers to the *overall impression a user* gathers from engaging with a website or a mobile app. I define "interaction" and "usage" in a broad sense, including elements like viewing, touching, and reflecting on the product, which covers its display before physical engagement, usability, usefulness, emotional effects during use, and the memories formed afterwards. All these factors fall under the umbrella of "interaction" and "usage context."

Is user experience purely an internal sensation for the user? What about the performance-related dimensions of usability? Certainly, users have internal *experiences influenced* by these factors, such as increased productivity. However, there are also observable indicators of usability, like the time taken to complete tasks, which users might not consciously recognize or associate with their emotions. The same holds for usefulness. If I consider usability and usefulness as components of user experience, it stands to reason that not every element of user experience is subjectively perceived.

When I refer to "usability," I usually mean the practical and objective aspects of the user experience. This includes measurable performance metrics and users' subjective opinions, along with qualitative insights into usability challenges. In contrast, "user experience" describes the internal feelings of the user, integrating the effects of usability, usefulness, and emotional reactions.

User Experience Data from Websites: Ingest, Analyze, Improve, Connect

Page View Data

Reviewing the page view counts for different pages on your website can provide valuable insights, particularly when examined over time or across various site versions. For instance, consider a page dedicated to Product A that averaged 200 daily views in one month. After enhancing the homepage to better link to Product A's page, the next month saw an increase to an average of 400 daily views for that page. This suggests that modifications to the homepage likely led to a substantial rise in traffic to the Product A page. Nonetheless, it's essential to remain vigilant and verify that no other factors influenced this increase. In the public sector, certain pages may experience seasonal fluctuations in views; for example, a page about UK tax return submissions often sees heightened traffic just before January 31 due to the approaching deadline.

Your website might attract more visitors for various reasons, which can be advantageous. However, this increase may also be influenced by external factors unrelated to your site's design or usability, such as news events relevant to your topic. It's crucial to understand the role of search bots in your site's statistics. Search bots, or spiders, are automated tools used by major search engines to explore the web, following links and indexing the pages they encounter. A significant challenge that arises when your site gains popularity and is indexed by leading search engines is distinguishing actual page views from those generated by these search bots. Most bots (like Google and Yahoo!) typically identify themselves during page requests, allowing you to filter them out of your data.

What analyses can help ascertain whether one set of page views notably differs from another? Refer to Table 6-1, which presents the daily page views for a specific page over two weeks. Week 1 represents the period before the launch of a new homepage containing a revised link to the specific page, while Week 2 occurs after the launch.

Table 6-1. *Number of Page Views for a*
Web Page over Two Different Weeks

	Week 1	Week 2
Sun	200	300
Mon	500	600
Tue	400	500
Wed	600	700
Thu	550	650
Fri	500	600
Sat	300	350
Average	436	529

Week 1 occurred prior to the launch of the new homepage, while Week 2 followed it. The updated homepage featured different wording for the link to this page.

To analyze this data, a paired t-test is used to assess whether the average for Week 2 (529) differs significantly from that of Week 1 (436). Utilizing a paired t-test is essential because it reduces variability related to the days of the week; comparing each day to its corresponding day from the previous week helps mitigate this variability. The results of the paired t-test show that the difference is statistically significant ($p < 0.01$). If a t-test for two independent samples had been conducted instead, the outcome ($p = 0.19$) would not indicate any significant difference.

Drop-Off Rates Data

Drop-off rates are a useful indicator of possible usability problems on your site. They are typically employed to identify the exact pages from which users are exiting or abandoning tasks, like document creation or purchase completion. For example, if a user needs to fill out information across nine pages to create a certificate for fish export, Table 6-2 shows the percentage of users who initiated the process and successfully completed each of the nine webpages.

Table 6-2. *Percentage of Users Who Started a Multipage Process That Actually Completed Each of the Steps*

Page	% of users who completed the step
Login	72%
Find Category	65%
Create Document	55%
Read Document	52%
Add to Cart	45%
Update Address	42%
Checkout	30%
Check Status	25%

In this example, all percentages reflect the number of users who initiated the complete process, meaning those who reached Page #1, the login page. Therefore, 72% of users who reached Page #1 successfully completed it, 65% of that initial group finished Page #2, Find Category, and so forth. Referring to the data in Table 6-2, which page seems to present the most challenges for users? To determine this, examine how many users dropped off at each page—this indicates the difference between those who arrived at the page and those who completed it. The drop-off percentages for each page are detailed in Table 6-3.

Table 6-3. *Drop-Off Percentages for Each Page Shown in Table 6-2*

Page	% of users who completed the step	Drop-off Rate
Login	72%	28%
Find Category	65%	7%
Create Document	55%	10%
Read Document	52%	3%
Add to Cart	45%	7%
Update Address	42%	3%
Checkout	30%	12%
Check Status	25%	5%

This makes it clear that the largest drop-off rate, 28%, is associated with the Login page. If you're going to redesign this multipage process, you would be well advised to learn what's causing the drop-off at Login page and then try to address that in the redesign.

A/B Tests

A/B tests are a specific kind of live-site study where elements of webpages are altered for users. The usual method of A/B testing on a site involves displaying two different designs for a particular page or its elements. Some visitors encounter the "A" version, while others view the "B" version. Often, this assignment is randomized, resulting in a roughly equal number of visitors for each version. In certain situations, most visitors see the current page, while a smaller group is exposed to a new experimental design under test. Although these studies are commonly referred to as A/B tests, they can also involve multiple alternative designs for a page.

A successful A/B test necessitates thorough planning. Here are some essential tips to consider:

- Ensure that the method used to "split" visitors between the "A" and "B" versions is genuinely random. If someone suggests that it's sufficient to direct all morning visitors to version "A" and all afternoon visitors to version "B," don't buy into it. Morning and afternoon visitors might behave differently.

- Initially, test small changes. While it might be appealing to create two vastly different versions of a page, you will gain more insights from testing minor variations. If the versions differ significantly and one outperforms the other, you may not understand why. However, if the only distinction is the wording of the call-to-action button, you can clearly attribute any performance difference to that.

- Assess significance. A version might appear to outperform the other, but conducting a statistical test (e.g., $\chi 2$) is necessary to confirm this.

- Trust the data. The outcomes of A/B tests can often be surprising and counterintuitive. One of the benefits that UX researchers provide is the ability to further investigate these unexpected results through other methods (e.g., surveys, laboratory, or online studies) for deeper understanding.

Visitors to a page can be directed to one of the alternative pages through various methods, such as random number generation, the exact time (for instance, whether the number of seconds since midnight is even or odd), or other techniques. Usually, a cookie is created to record which version the visitor experienced, ensuring that if they return within a specified time frame, they will see the same version again. It's crucial to test the alternative versions simultaneously due to the external factors previously mentioned, as testing at different times could skew the results.

Well-structured A/B tests can provide valuable insights into what works and what doesn't work on your website. Numerous companies, such as Amazon, eBay, Google, Microsoft, Facebook, and others, regularly conduct A/B tests on their active sites, although most users remain unaware of it (Kohavi, Crook, & Longbotham, 2009; Kohavi, Deng, Frasca, Longbotham, Walker, & Xu, 2012; Tang, Agarwal, O'Brien, & Meyer, 2010). Indeed, Kohavi and Round (2004) noted that A/B testing is a continuous process at Amazon, where experimentation through A/B testing is the primary method for site modifications.

Summary

Insights delivered by GA4 need the help of UX professionals to bring about meaningful change, which will transform business performance by emotionally affecting the users. One main area where this change happens is the user experience on a website. Various design qualities influence the user experience on a website, extending beyond usability. I prefer to refer to it as "visitor experience" when designing a web user interface. Additionally, I acknowledge that at least five distinct website qualities can affect visitors' experiences:

1. Utility

2. Functional integrity

3. Usability

4. Persuasiveness

5. Graphic design

Although utility and functional integrity are mainly separate design qualities, the distinctions among usability, persuasiveness, and graphic design are less clear. Both usability and well-executed graphic design can enhance persuasiveness, and graphic design also plays a crucial role in usability. However, analyzing these qualities separately can aid in understanding their significance and applying them effectively throughout the design process.

Creating an exceptional visitor experience demands a specialized tea*m. Market research,* a longstanding discipline, plays a vital role in ensuring *usefulness.* Skilled w*eb develope*rs are essential for maintaining *functional integrity.* Expertise in s*oftware and web usability engineering* is key to enhancing *user experience. Recently*, a new generation of professionals has begun integrating marketing and *persuasion psychology* into e-commerce website design. Additionally, *graphic design*ers focused on website design provide crucial skills in branding and audience engagement, which are vital for websites.

Success depends on forming a strong interdisciplinary design team, not just choosing skilled individuals. Professionals from diverse fields often lack a thorough understanding of each other's expertise, which can reduce collaboration effectiveness in creating the best visitor experience for a specific audience. At the very least, stakeholders should ensure that product development team members value each other's skills and are open to learning, fostering collaboration focused on designing an optimal experience for website visitors. By leveraging their diverse knowledge, experts from various backgrounds can significantly boost website success and deliver a positive experience for the target audience.

CHAPTER 7

Measuring User Behavior and Improving Business Performance

Senior managers and key stakeholders in a project typically focus on performance metrics, particularly when presented well. They are interested in how many users can successfully complete essential tasks with a product. These performance metrics are viewed as significant indicators of usability and potential predictors of cost savings and revenue growth.

Every technology user must engage with an interface to achieve their objectives. For instance, a website user clicks on various links, a word-processing application user types in information using a keyboard, or a video game player presses buttons on a remote control or moves a controller in the air. Regardless of the technology, users interact with a product in a specific manner. These interactions are fundamental to business performance metrics.

All types of user behavior can be measured in various ways. Behaviors that fulfill a user's goals significantly impact their experience. For instance, you can track whether users navigating through a website found what they were searching for. You can also assess the time it takes for users to enter and format a page of text accurately in a word processor, or count how many buttons users press while cooking a frozen meal in a microwave. Performance metrics are derived from these specific user behaviors.

Performance metrics depend not just on user behaviors but also on defined scenarios or tasks. For example, to effectively measure success, users need to have specific tasks or goals in mind, such as finding the price of a sweatshirt or submitting a tax return. Performance metrics are not viable without these tasks; simply browsing a website or experimenting with software doesn't provide a clear measure of success. How can you determine if the user was successful in such cases? However, tasks don't have to be arbitrary; they can reflect what users aim to accomplish on a live website or emerge from participants in a usability study. Often, we orient our studies around fundamental tasks.

Performance metrics serve as crucial tools for usability professionals, providing the best means to assess the effectiveness and efficiency of various products. When users encounter numerous errors, it highlights areas needing improvement. Additionally, if users take four times longer than anticipated to complete a task, there are significant opportunities to enhance efficiency. Ultimately, performance metrics are essential for understanding how effectively users engage with a product.

Performance metrics help gauge the scale of specific usability problems. It's often insufficient to simply identify a usability issue; understanding how many users might face the same challenge post-release is crucial. For instance, calculating a success rate along with a confidence interval can provide a sound estimate of the severity of a usability issue. By assessing task completion times, you can identify the percentage of your target audience that can finish a task within a designated time frame. If only 15% of targeted users succeed in completing a specific task, it clearly indicates a usability issue.

Performance metrics aren't a one-size-fits-all solution. Like other metrics, they require a sufficient sample size. While statistics can be applied with as few as five users or as many as 500, your level of confidence will vary significantly with the sample size. If your goal is simply to pinpoint the most severe issues with a product, then investing in performance metrics might not be the best use of resources. However, should you aim for a more detailed assessment and can gather data from ten or more users, you will likely achieve meaningful performance metrics with a reasonable degree of confidence.

Minimize reliance on performance metrics if your aim is to reveal fundamental usability issues. When measuring task success or completion time, it's easy to overlook the real problems behind the figures. Performance metrics effectively convey the what but fail to explain the why. While performance data can highlight tasks or interface elements that troubled users, it does not pinpoint the root causes of these issues. Therefore, it's essential to complement it with additional information, like observational or self-reported data, to gain a clearer understanding of why these issues occurred and how they can be resolved.

Types of User Behavior Performance Metrics

Usability is like love. You have to care, you have to listen, and you have to be willing to change. You will make mistakes along the way, but that's where growth and forgiveness come in.

—Jeffrey Zeldman

Some professionals differentiate between the terms usability and user experience. Usability typically refers to how effectively a user can utilize a product to accomplish a task, while user experience encompasses a more comprehensive perspective, considering the overall interaction of the individual with the product, along with the thoughts, emotions, and perceptions that arise from that engagement.

In casual discussions on usability, most would concur that an effective, user-friendly design is preferable. Conversely, a few companies might intentionally create confusing or frustrating products, though such instances are uncommon. For this book, we will adopt a somewhat idealistic view, assuming that both users and designers strive for products that are easy to use, efficient, and engaging.

Prioritizing user experience in business typically focuses on boosting revenue and cutting costs. Numerous stories highlight businesses that suffered financial losses due to the inadequate user experience of a new product. Conversely, some companies have positioned ease of use as a central element of their brand identity.

User experience is playing an increasingly vital role in our lives as products grow more complex. With the evolution and maturation of technologies, their user base becomes more diverse. However, this escalation in complexity does not automatically translate to greater ease of use; in fact, the opposite can occur if we neglect user experience. As technology becomes more intricate, we believe it is essential to prioritize user experience and incorporate UX metrics into the development process, ensuring that advanced technology remains efficient, user-friendly, and engaging.

This chapter discusses three primary types of performance metrics:

1. Time on task is a standard metric used to gauge the duration needed to finish a task.

2. Task success is arguably the most prevalent performance metric, measuring how well users can complete a specified set of tasks. This includes two variations: binary success and varying levels of success, as well as the option to assess task failures.

3. Efficiency is evaluated by considering how much effort users put into completing a task, including metrics like the number of clicks on a website or button presses on a mobile device.

Time on Task

Time on task, often called task completion time or simply task time, is an effective measure of a product's efficiency. Generally, the quicker a user can finish a task, the better their experience. It's rare for users to voice complaints about a task taking less time than anticipated. However, there are exceptions to the notion that faster is always preferable. In gaming, for instance, players usually prefer not to rush through the experience. The key goal for most games is to enjoy the experience rather than to complete tasks quickly. E-learning also presents exceptions; for instance, in developing an online training course, a slower pace may be advantageous. Users are likely to retain information better if they take their time completing tasks instead of hurrying through the material.

My claim that quicker task completion is preferable contrasts with the perspective from web analytics, which suggests that increased page views or session durations are desirable. From the web analytics viewpoint, longer page-view durations (the time each user spends viewing individual pages) and extended session durations (the total time users spend on the site) are usually seen as positive metrics. This is because they signify higher levels of "engagement" with the site, making it appear more "sticky." The reason my assertion seems to conflict with this viewpoint is that I don't concur with it. Metrics like session and page-view duration reflect the site owner's perspective, rather than that of the user. I maintain that users generally prefer to spend *less* time on a site, rather than *more*. However, there may be a way to align these two viewpoints. Perhaps a key objective for a site could be encouraging users to engage in more thorough or complex tasks, instead of just superficial ones. More intricate tasks typically result in longer times spent on the site *and* increased task durations compared to simpler tasks.

Time on task holds significant importance for products involving repetitive user actions. For instance, when creating a website for customer service representatives at a travel company, the duration required to finalize a web reservation serves as a key efficiency metric. The quicker a travel agent can make a reservation, the more web chat requests they can manage, ultimately leading to enhanced cost savings. As a user performs a task more frequently, the value of efficiency escalates. A notable advantage of tracking time on task is its relative ease in calculating cost savings from efficiency improvements, enabling the derivation of a tangible return on investment (ROI).

Table 7-1. *Time-on-Task Data for 10 Participants and 5 Tasks (All Data Are Expressed in Seconds)*

Task Time	Login	Navigate	Search	Find Category	Create Document	Average
Participant 1	80	120	110	100	156	113.2
Participant 2	67	143	100	110	164	116.8
Participant 3	72	110	95	85	145	101.4
Participant 4	35	99	84	74	135	85.4
Participant 5	45	82	77	70	130	80.8
Participant 6	55	120	85	80	180	104
Participant 7	52	122	99	110	155	107.6
Participant 8	64	112	112	72	165	105
Participant 9	77	95	120	85	155	106.4
Participant 10	82	100	75	120	185	112.4
Average	62.9	110.3	95.7	90.6	157	103.3
StdDev	15.7653	17.2114	15.3482	18.0321	17.6131	
90% Confidence interval	8.2003	8.9525	7.9833	9.3794	9.1614	
Upper Bound	71.1	119.3	103.7	100.0	166.2	
Lower Bound	54.7	101.3	87.7	81.2	147.8	

There are various methods to analyze and present time-on-task data. The most common approach is to examine the average time users spend on specific tasks, calculated by averaging individual times for each task (see Figure 7-1). This method is clear and easy to understand. However, one drawback is the potential variability among different users. For instance, if several users take an unusually long time to complete a task, the overall average may be skewed. Therefore, it is essential to include a confidence interval to illustrate the variability in the time data. This will not only reflect the differences within the same task but also help to visualize discrepancies between tasks, aiding in the assessment of whether there are statistically significant differences among them.

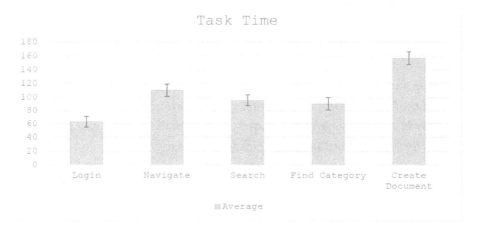

Figure 7-1. *Mean time on task, in seconds, for 5 tasks. Error bars represent a 90% confidence interval. These data are from an online study of a prototype website*

At times, it's better to present time-on-task data using the median instead of the mean. The median represents the midpoint in a sequential list of all recorded times: half the times fall below this point and half above it. Likewise, the geometric mean may offer less bias compared to the mean. Since time data often display skewness, the median or geometric mean are generally more suitable options. In practice, we observe that employing these alternative methods for summarizing time data can alter the overall time values, but the types of patterns you care about (like task comparisons) tend to remain consistent; the same tasks typically exhibit the longest or shortest durations overall.

One method of calculating the average completion time by task is to establish ranges, or specific time intervals, and then report how many users fall into each interval. This approach effectively visualizes the distribution of completion times among all users. Additionally, it can help identify patterns among users in specific segments. For instance, you might focus on users with notably long completion times to determine if they have any shared characteristics.

A key consideration is whether to include timestamps for only the successful tasks or for all tasks in your analysis. The primary benefit of focusing solely on successful tasks is that it provides a clearer measure of efficiency. For instance, estimating time data for unsuccessful tasks can be quite challenging. Some users may continue their attempts until the computer is nearly unplugged. Consequently, any task that concludes with either the participant giving up or the moderator intervening will yield highly variable time data.

One key benefit of assessing time data for every task, whether successful or not, is that it provides a more precise representation of the user experience as a whole. For instance, if only a small percentage of users succeed, but that group is exceptionally efficient, the average time spent on tasks will seem low. This can lead to misinterpretations of time-on-task data when focusing solely on successful tasks. Additionally, evaluating time data across all tasks serves as an independent metric compared to task success data. Limiting the analysis to successful tasks creates a reliance between these two datasets.

A helpful guideline is that if the participant consistently determined when to abandon unsuccessful tasks, all instances should be included in the analysis. In cases where the moderator occasionally decided when to conclude an unsuccessful task, only consider the times for successful tasks.

Task Success

Task success stands as the most prevalent usability metric, applicable to nearly any usability study involving tasks. This metric is nearly universal, as it can be calculated across diverse *items* being tested, ranging from websites to mobile phones. So long as the user has a clearly defined task, success can be measured.

Task success is universally relatable. It's not necessary to delve into complex measurement methods or statistics to convey this. If users struggle to finish their tasks, it's clear that an issue exists. Witnessing users unable to complete a simple task serves as strong proof that something requires attention.

To evaluate task success, each user task must have a defined objective, such as buying a product, locating a specific answer, or filling out an online application. It's essential to specify what success looks like by establishing clear success criteria for each task before you begin data collection. Failing to outline these criteria in advance may lead to poorly formulated tasks and unreliable success data. Below are examples of tasks with both clear and ambiguous end states:

- Find the 5-year gain or loss for Apple stock (clear end state).

- Research ways to save for your retirement (not a clear end state).

Although the second task may be perfectly appropriate in certain types of usability studies, it's not appropriate for measuring task success.

The typical method for assessing success in a lab-based usability test involves having the user verbally express their answer after finishing the task. While this approach feels natural for the user, it can occasionally lead to responses that are hard to interpret. Users might provide excessive or unrelated details, complicating the interpretation of their answers. In such cases, probing the users may be necessary to ensure they truly completed the task successfully.

Another effective method for gathering success data is to have users respond in a more structured format, such as through an online tool or a printed form. Each task can include multiple-choice options, allowing users to select the correct answer from a list of four to five distractors. It's crucial to ensure that the distractors are realistic. If possible, avoid open-ended write-in responses, as they require more time for analysis and may lead to subjective interpretations, introducing additional variability to the data.

Binary success is the most straightforward and commonly used method for assessing task success. Users either accomplish a task or they do not, similar to a "pass/fail" course in a university. This approach is suitable when the success of a product hinges on users completing a specific task or series of tasks; merely coming close is not enough. The key factor is achieving the intended goal through their tasks. For instance, consider a task aimed at purchasing a shirt online. While it may be useful to identify where a user encountered difficulties, if your company relies on selling those shirts, that is what truly matters.

Whenever users complete a task, they should receive a score indicating either "success" or "failure." Usually, these scores are represented with 1's (for success) and 0's (for failure). It's easier to analyze data using numeric values instead of textual representations like "success" or "failure." By adopting a numeric scoring system, you can easily compute the percentage of correct attempts along with any additional statistics you may require. To find the percentage correct, calculate the average of the 1's and 0's. If you have multiple participants and tasks, there are always two methods to assess task success:

- By examining the average success rate for each *task among* the participants

- By examining the average success rate for each *participant* across the tasks

For instance, refer to the data displayed in Table 7-2. The averages at the bottom indicate the task success rates for each *task*, while the averages on the right show the success rates for each *participant*. Provided there are no missing data, the averages of these two sets will always be equivalent.

Table 7-2. *Task Success Data for 10 Participants and 10 Tasks*

Task Success	Login	Navigate	Search	Find Category	Create Document	Read Document	Add to Cart	Update Address	Checkout	Check Status	Average
Participant 1	1	1	1	1	1	1	1	1	0	1	90%
Participant 2	1	0	1	1	0	1	1	0	0	1	60%
Participant 3	1	1	0	0	0	1	1	0	0	0	40%
Participant 4	1	0	0	0	1	0	1	1	0	0	40%
Participant 5	0	0	1	0	1	1	0	0	0	0	30%
Participant 6	1	1	1	1	0	0	1	1	1	1	80%
Participant 7	0	1	1	0	0	1	1	1	0	1	60%
Participant 8	0	0	0	0	0	0	0	0	0	1	10%
Participant 9	1	0	0	0	0	1	1	1	0	1	50%
Participant 10	1	1	0	1	0	1	1	1	0	1	70%
Average	70%	50%	50%	40%	30%	70%	80%	60%	10%	70%	53%
StdDev	0.4830	0.5270	0.5270	0.5164	0.4830	0.4830	0.4216	0.5164	0.3162	0.4830	
90% Confidence interval	0.2513	0.2741	0.2741	0.2686	0.2513	0.2513	0.2193	0.2686	0.1645	0.2513	

The typical method for analyzing and presenting binary success rates is by task, which involves showing the percentage of participants who successfully completed each task. Figure 7-2 illustrates the task success rates corresponding to the data in Table 7-2. This method is particularly effective for comparing success rates across different tasks. Subsequent detailed analyses can focus on specific issues to identify necessary changes. For instance, Figure 7-2 indicates that the tasks "Create Document" and "Checkout" are likely to encounter difficulties.

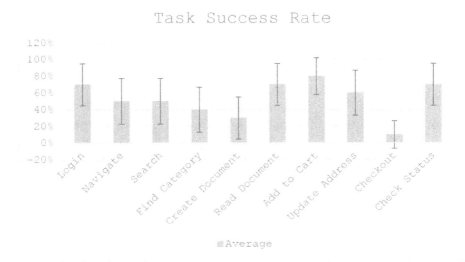

Figure 7-2. *Task success rates for the data in Table 7-2, including a 90% confidence interval for each task*

A typical approach to assessing binary success is by focusing on the user or user type. When reporting usability data, it's essential to ensure user anonymity by using numbers or nonidentifiable descriptors. Analyzing success data from the user standpoint enables the identification of distinct user groups that either perform differently or face varying challenges. Below are four common methods for segmenting users:

1. Usage frequency (infrequent vs. frequent users)

2. Prior experience with the product

3. Expertise level (low vs. high domain knowledge)

4. Age category

A crucial aspect of analyzing and presenting binary success is the inclusion of confidence intervals. These intervals are vital as they indicate your level of trust in the data. In many usability studies, binary success

144

data often arise from relatively small sample sizes (e.g., 5 to 20 users). As a result, the binary success metric might not be as dependable as desired. For instance, if 4 out of 5 users managed to complete a task successfully, how certain can we be that 80% of a larger user population will also accomplish the same task? Clearly, our confidence would increase if 16 out of 20 users completed the task, and even more so if 80 out of 100 users did so.

Efficiency

Time on task is commonly used to gauge efficiency, but another method is to assess the effort needed to accomplish a task. This is often achieved by counting the number of actions or steps users take to perform each task. Actions can vary widely, including clicking a link on a web page, pressing a button on a microwave or mobile device, or flipping a switch on an aircraft. Each action signifies a certain level of effort; thus, a higher number of actions indicates greater effort. Typically, in most products, the aim is to enhance productivity by reducing the number of discrete actions required to complete a task, which in turn lessens the overall effort involved.

What do we mean by effort? There are primarily two types: cognitive and physical. Cognitive effort includes identifying the appropriate location to perform an action (e.g., locating a link on a web page), determining what action is needed (should I click this link?), and understanding the consequences of that action. Physical effort refers to the actual physical activities required to take action, such as moving the mouse, typing on a keyboard, flipping a switch, among others.

Efficiency metrics are effective when considering not only the time required to complete a task, but also the cognitive and physical effort involved. For instance, when designing a car navigation system, it is crucial to ensure that interpreting the navigation directions requires minimal effort, as the driver's primary focus should remain on the road. Therefore, reducing both cognitive and physical effort needed to use the navigation system is essential.

Several key points should be considered when gathering and assessing efficiency.

- *Determine the Actions to Measure:* For websites, typical actions include mouse clicks and page views. In software, you might track mouse clicks or keystrokes. For appliances and consumer electronics, button presses are relevant. No matter the product being assessed, ensure you have a comprehensive understanding of all potential actions.

- *Identify the Initiation and Conclusion of an Action:* It is essential to recognize when an action starts and finishes. Some actions, like pressing a button, occur swiftly, while others can be extended over a longer time frame. Actions can also be more passive, such as viewing a web page. Certain actions have a distinct beginning and end, while others are more ambiguous.

- *Track the Actions:* It's essential to track the actions clearly. They should occur at a visual pace, or if too rapid, be identifiable by an automated system. Aim to eliminate the need for reviewing hours of footage to gather efficiency metrics.

- *Actions Should Hold Significance:* Every action needs to signify an incremental rise in cognitive and physical effort. Increased actions correspond to heightened effort. For instance, each mouse click typically indicates a small increase in effort.

After identifying the actions to track, counting them becomes straightforward. You can do this manually, for instance, by tallying page views or button presses. While this method can work for simpler products, it's often impractical in most situations. Participants frequently perform these actions rapidly, sometimes exceeding multiple actions per second. Therefore, utilizing automated data collection tools like Google Analytics is much more advantageous.

The most prevalent method for analyzing and presenting efficiency metrics involves examining the number of actions each participant executes to complete a task. To find the average number of actions taken per participant for each task, simply perform the calculation. This analysis proves beneficial in pinpointing which tasks demand the most effort; it is particularly effective when each task requires a similar number of actions. However, this approach may yield misleading results if certain tasks are significantly more complex than others. Additionally, it is crucial to include the confidence intervals, which are derived from a continuous distribution, in this type of task.

Another perspective on efficiency views it as a combination of two metrics outlined in this chapter: task success and time on task. The Common Industry Format for Usability Test Reports (ISO/IEC 25062:2006) defines the "core measure of efficiency" as the ratio of the task completion rate to the average time per task. In essence, it quantifies task success relative to time. Typically, time per task is measured in minutes, but seconds may be appropriate for very brief tasks or hours for exceptionally lengthy ones. The chosen time unit influences the scale of the results. It's important to select a unit that provides a "reasonable" scale (i.e., where most values range between 1 and 100%). Table 7-3 illustrates how to calculate an efficiency metric using task completion and task time, while Figure 7-3 presents this efficiency metric visually in a chart.

Table 7-3. *The Efficiency Measure Is Simply the Ratio of Task Completion to Task Time in Minutes*

Task	Task Success Rate	Task Time (min.)	Efficiency(%)
Login	70%	1.2	58%
Navigate	50%	1.6	31%
Search	50%	1.4	36%
Find Category	40%	1.5	27%
Create Document	30%	2.5	12%
Read Document	70%	2.1	33%
Add to Cart	80%	1.7	47%
Update Address	60%	1.4	43%
Checkout	10%	3.2	3%
Check Status	70%	2.3	30%

Certainly, increased efficiency is preferable. In this instance, users seem to have completed the "Login" and "Add to Cart" tasks more efficiently than the others.

Figure 7-3. *An example showing efficiency as a function of completion rate/time*

Summary

This book discusses how vision becomes goals, goals give way to objectives, objectives are transformed into performance measures, performance measures create the performance metrics, performance metrics are recorded and analyzed in Google Analytics, and finally, a better user experience is delivered, improving overall business performance. While writing this book, I felt as though I was witnessing the journey of a great river, from the mountain to the sea. I hope you will also appreciate the magnanimity of this journey and find enjoyment in reading this book. Good luck!

Index

GPSR Compliance
The European Union's (EU) General Product Safety Regulation (GPSR) is a set
of rules that requires consumer products to be safe and our obligations to
ensure this.

If you have any concerns about our products, you can contact us on

ProductSafety@springernature.com

In case Publisher is established outside the EU, the EU authorized
representative is:

Springer Nature Customer Service Center GmbH
Europaplatz 3
69115 Heidelberg, Germany